NO MAN'S LAND

Views from a Surveillance State

■■■■

Marcus DeSieno

Daylight

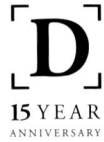

D

15 YEAR
ANNIVERSARY

Cofounders: Taj Forer and Michael Itkoff
Creative director: Ursula Damm
Copy editors: Nancy Hubbard, B. Richard

ISBN 978-1-942084-46-4

Printed by OFSET YAPIMEVI, Istanbul

Daylight Books
E-mail: info@daylightbooks.org
Web: www.daylightbooks.org

For Jaro and Lucy

Marcus DeSieno: Interrupt This Broadcast

By Ariel Shanberg

Nestled within the Olympian gaze of a remote surveillance apparatus, situated high above a seemingly innocuous wooded landscape, lies the question, "if a tree falls in the forest and there is no one to hear it, does it make a sound?"

That philosophical thought experiment, which pointedly reflects upon the tension between *observation* and *perception*, illustrates the fractured relationship we have today with the environment and echoes the camera's role in it. It permeates Marcus DeSieno's haunting images in *No Man's Land: Views from a Surveillance State* that confront the medium's increasing influence in distancing us from our surroundings by making them ever more visible.

Photography, as purposed by DeSieno's photographic forbearers, was a tool to chart the unseen. Their intent was to insert man into the undiscovered country, to lay claim to what was perceived as unpossessed. "Heroic" images declared vast wildernesses as both conquered and accessible. Fast-forward through multiple generations of technological advancements in photographic imaging and we find ourselves living in an age where the camera's impact in crafting our understanding of the world near and far—with its increasingly ubiquitous presence, accessibility, and autonomous abilities—is understood to be far from benign. Digital cameras, which can effortlessly record and transmit with unblinking consistency and hyper-real definition (and our willing nature to employ them to document and post any and every aspect of our lives), have deeply complicated our notions of public and private.

The medium's bifurcated tropes—as a means for discovery and a tool for establishing control—lie at the center of DeSieno's investigations. Embedded in this seemingly innocuous terrain, attributed only with a longitude and a latitude, is the fact that they are derived from surveillance cameras, public webcams, and CCTV feeds, which DeSieno hacked and culled from his computer. The surveilled landscapes that DeSieno isolates confront the notion of an all-seeing eye—one omnipresent in urban settings but startlingly invasive in these locales—have been used to enforce rules and articulate boundaries that are invisible to the naked eye. Where once the photograph proffered an invitation to explore, the endless feed of surveillance cameras brings forth declarations of restriction and implications of trespassing.

Confronted with omniscient video feeds, DeSieno employed the expansionist aesthetics associated with such photographers as Carleton Watkins, whose mammoth wet-plate images came to define the western American landscape as his editorial guides for discovering his images. On the surface, DeSieno's approach is a gesture toward the sublime. That is a misdirection, which he utilizes to disrupt the digital uniformity of his source material and its automated origins. The results engage our senses when negotiating his imagery. Brushstrokes of emulsion and grain evoke howling winds and swirling dust storms. Far from offering contained picture-perfect Kodak moments, DeSieno constructs eerie, affected terrains in which only the rare roadway suggests modern civilization's mark upon the landscape—nature's immensity and foreboding dominance pervades.

In blurring the boundaries between his source material and the aesthetics of those photographic geological surveys, DeSieno conflates the romanticized elements of photography's past with the sterile uniformity of modern imaging technologies and places his photographic works into a liminal space, where surface tension holds the images to scrutiny rather than romantic seduction.

In 1878, Eadweard Muybridge invented photographic technology to make motion studies of a horse in order to address what the human eye could not discern—whether or not there was a moment in a horse's stride in which all four of its feet were off the ground. The resulting images revolutionized our understanding of movement and photography's ability to help us see. As a young man, DeSieno used the money he won in a placed bet at a horse race in Saratoga Springs to purchase his first camera. It is a befitting origin for an artist so invested in addressing the camera's powers of observation and its influence on our perception. As with previous bodies of work in which he has utilized the dry-plate gelatin silver tintype process to reimagine images of microscopic parasites captured through an electron microscope as matinee-esque horror-film creatures, or cultivated imploding universes by inserting bacterial matter on color slides of galactic compositions, through his imaginative rerouting of representations of the unseen in *No Man's Land: Views from a Surveillance State,* DeSieno has brought our attention to the subjective and fragile nature of how we relate to the world before and beyond us through the camera.

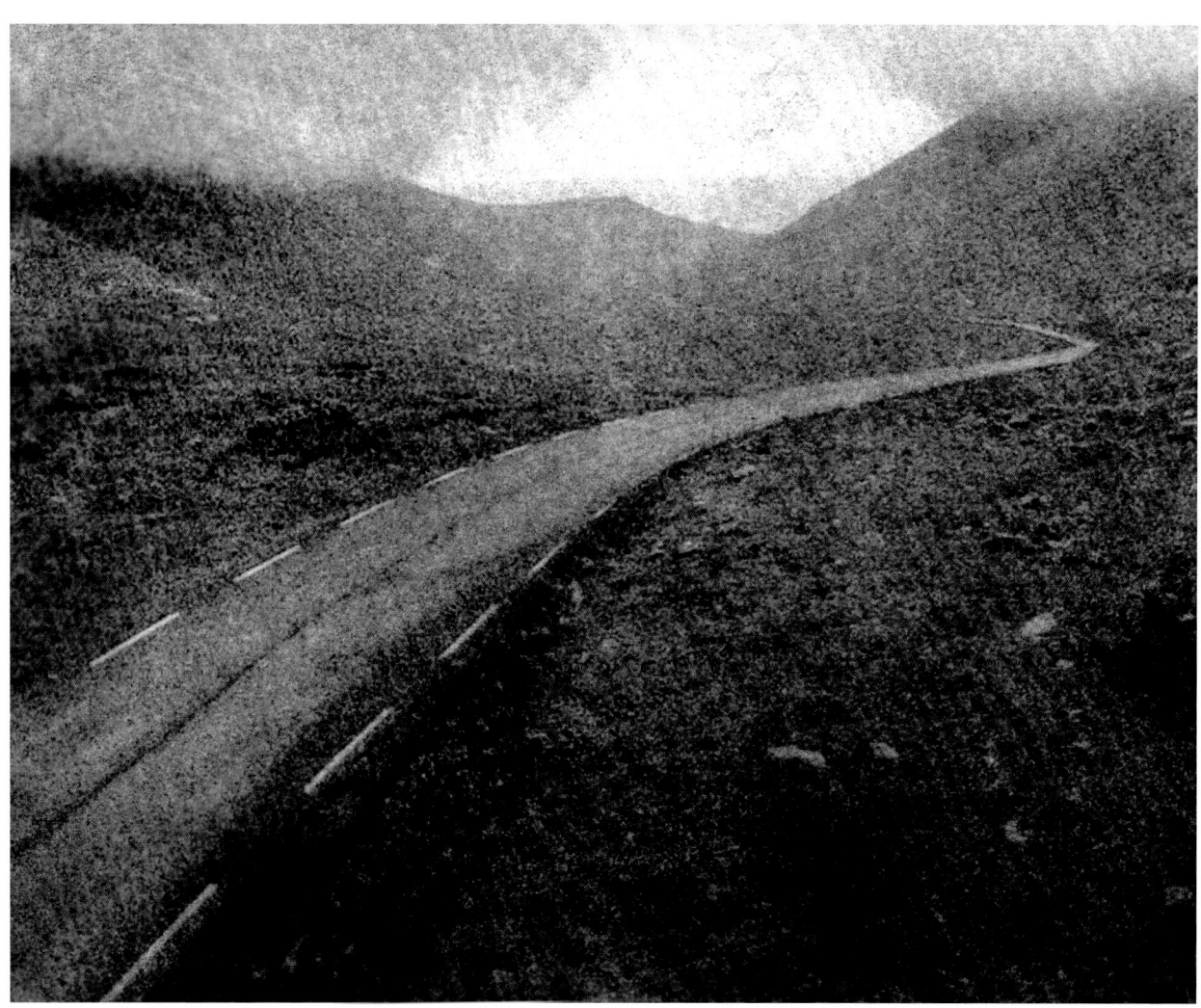

"We feel free because we lack the very language to articulate our unfreedom."

—— Slavoj Žižek, *Welcome to the Desert of the Real*

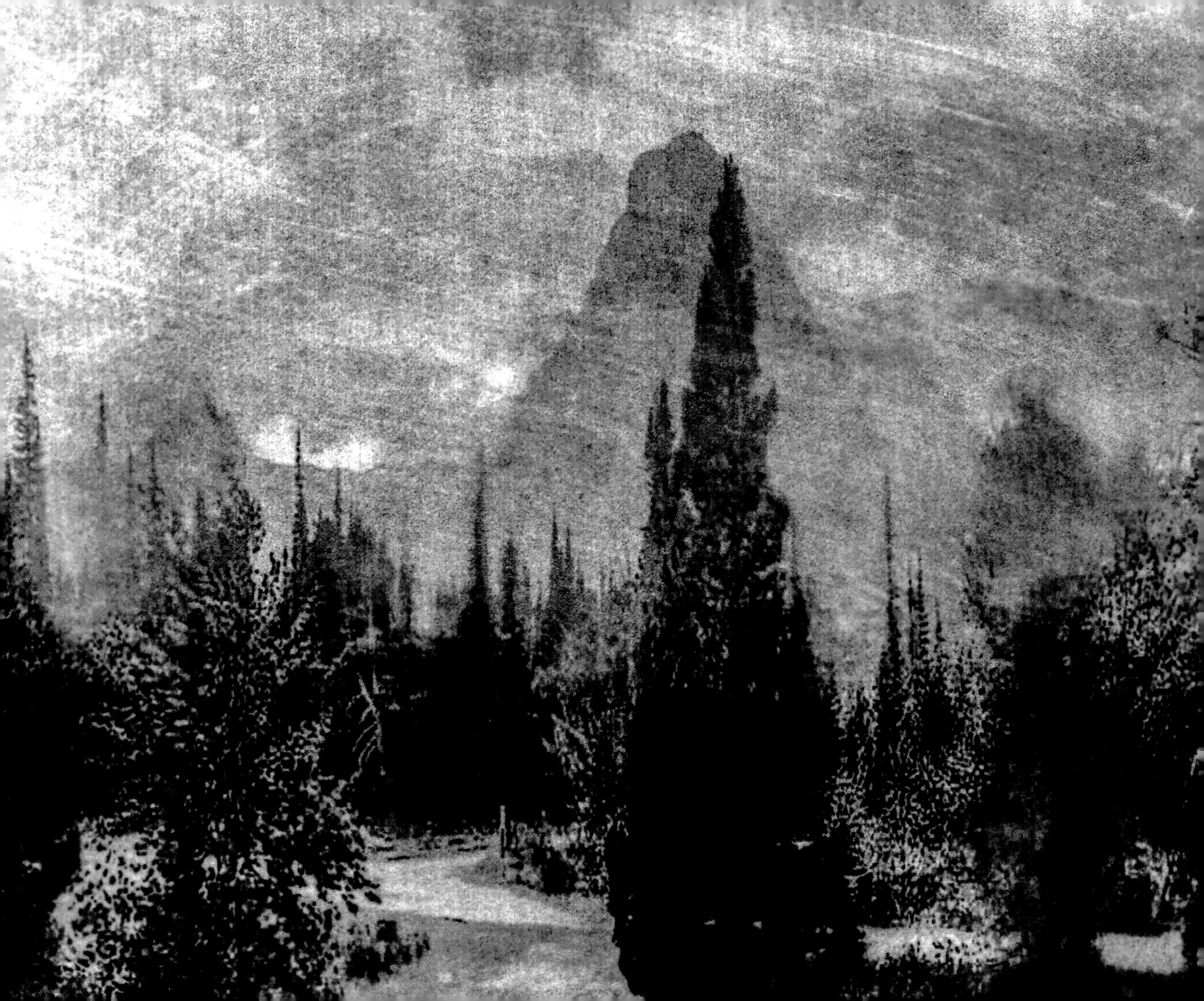

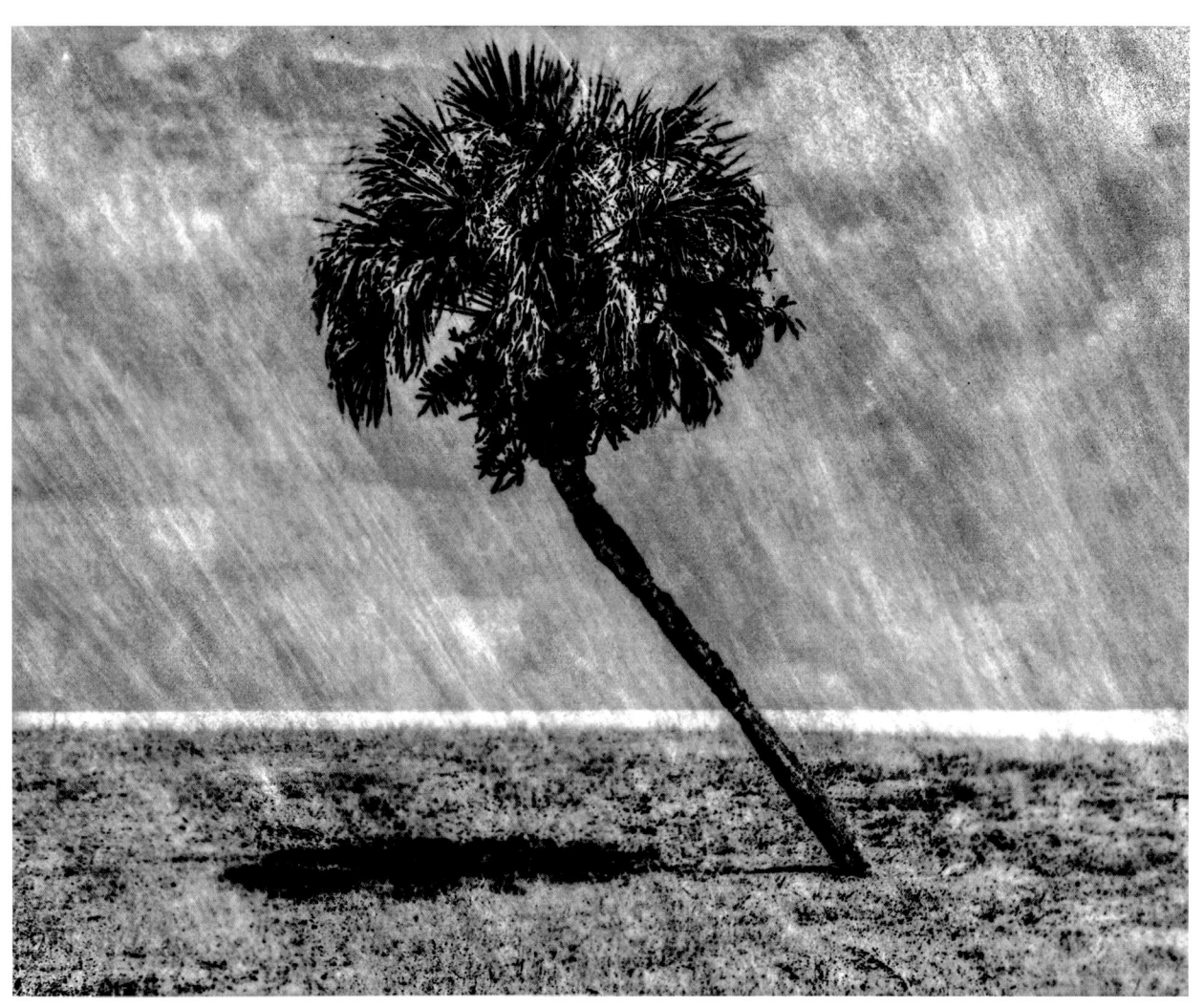

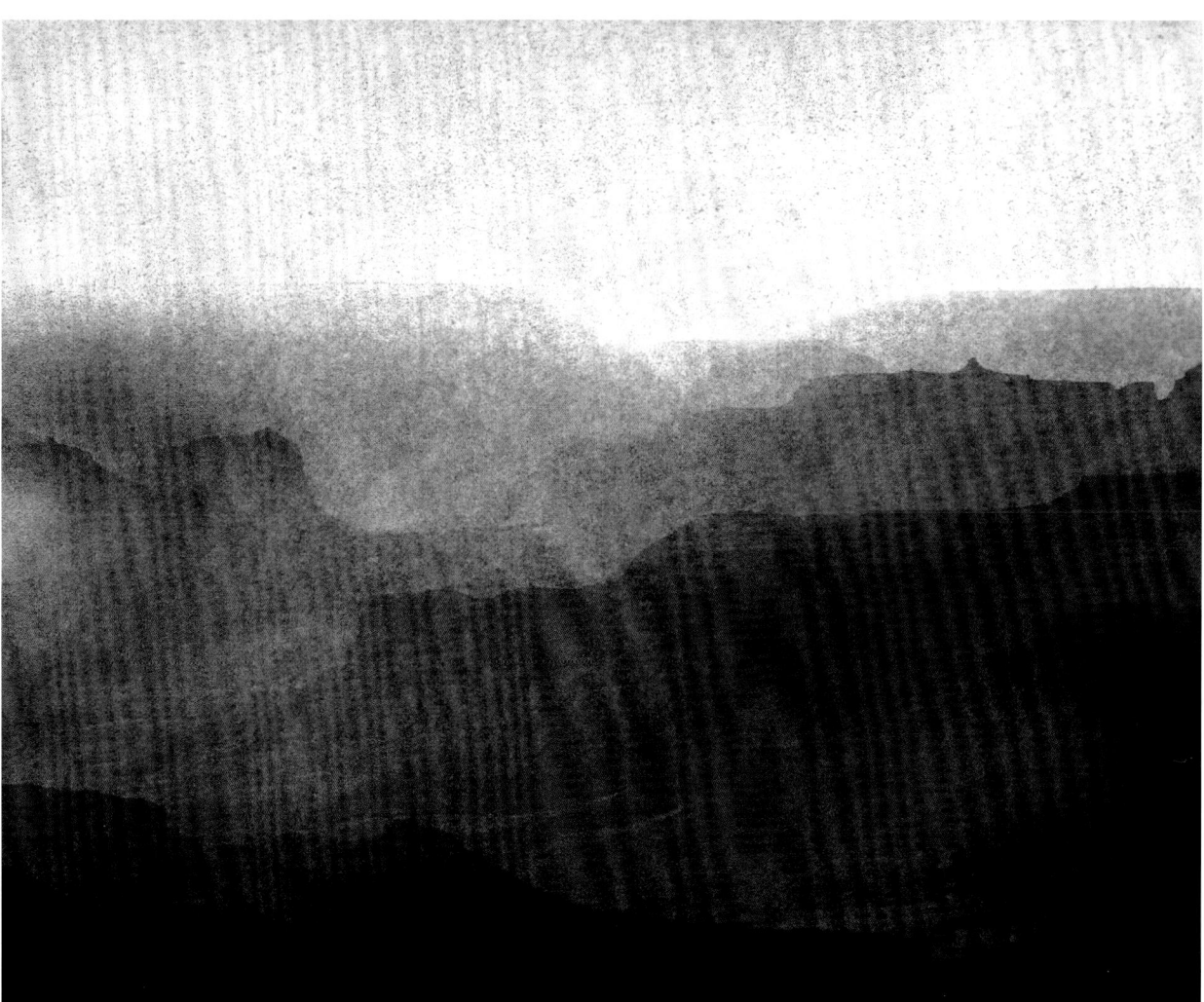

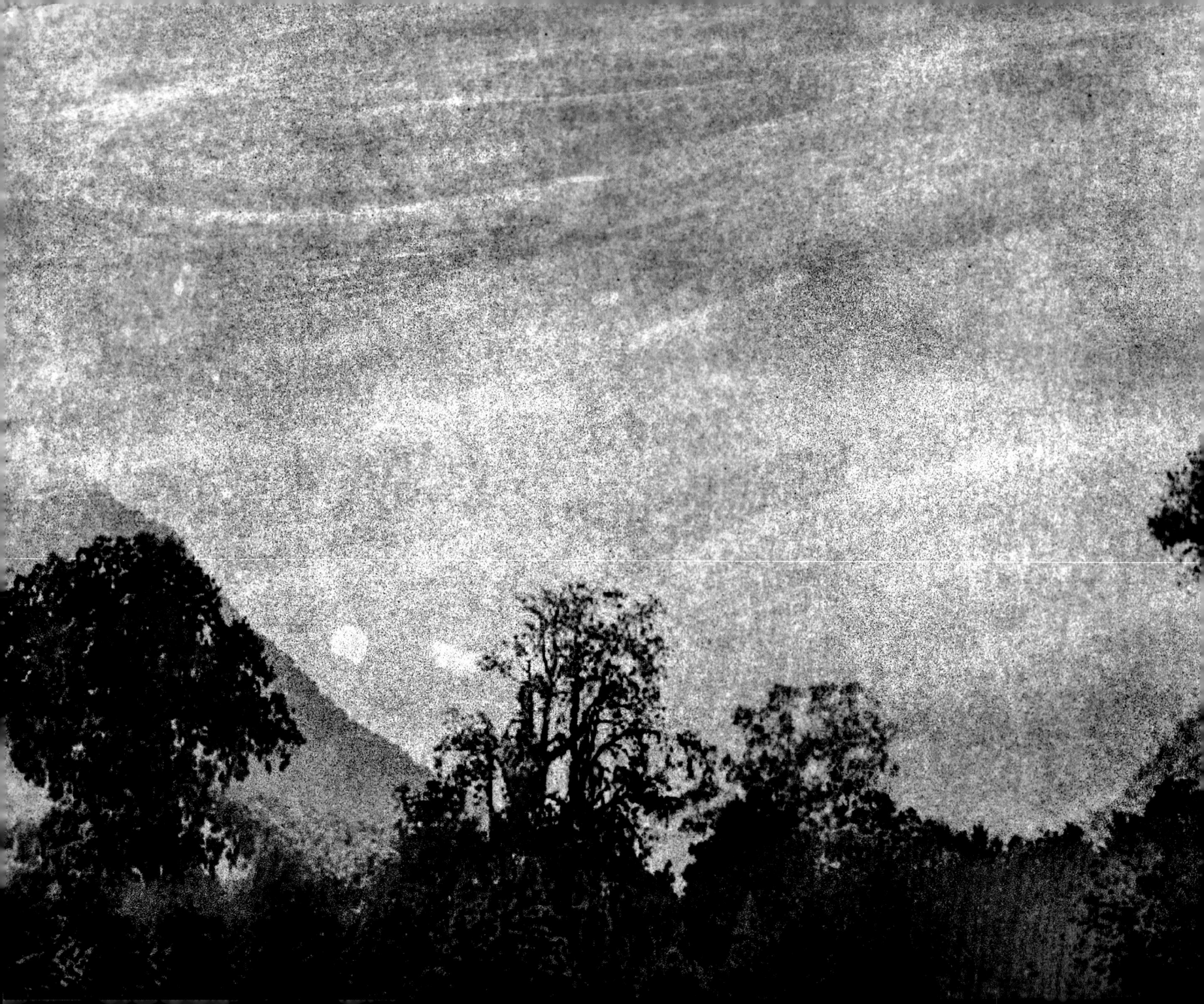

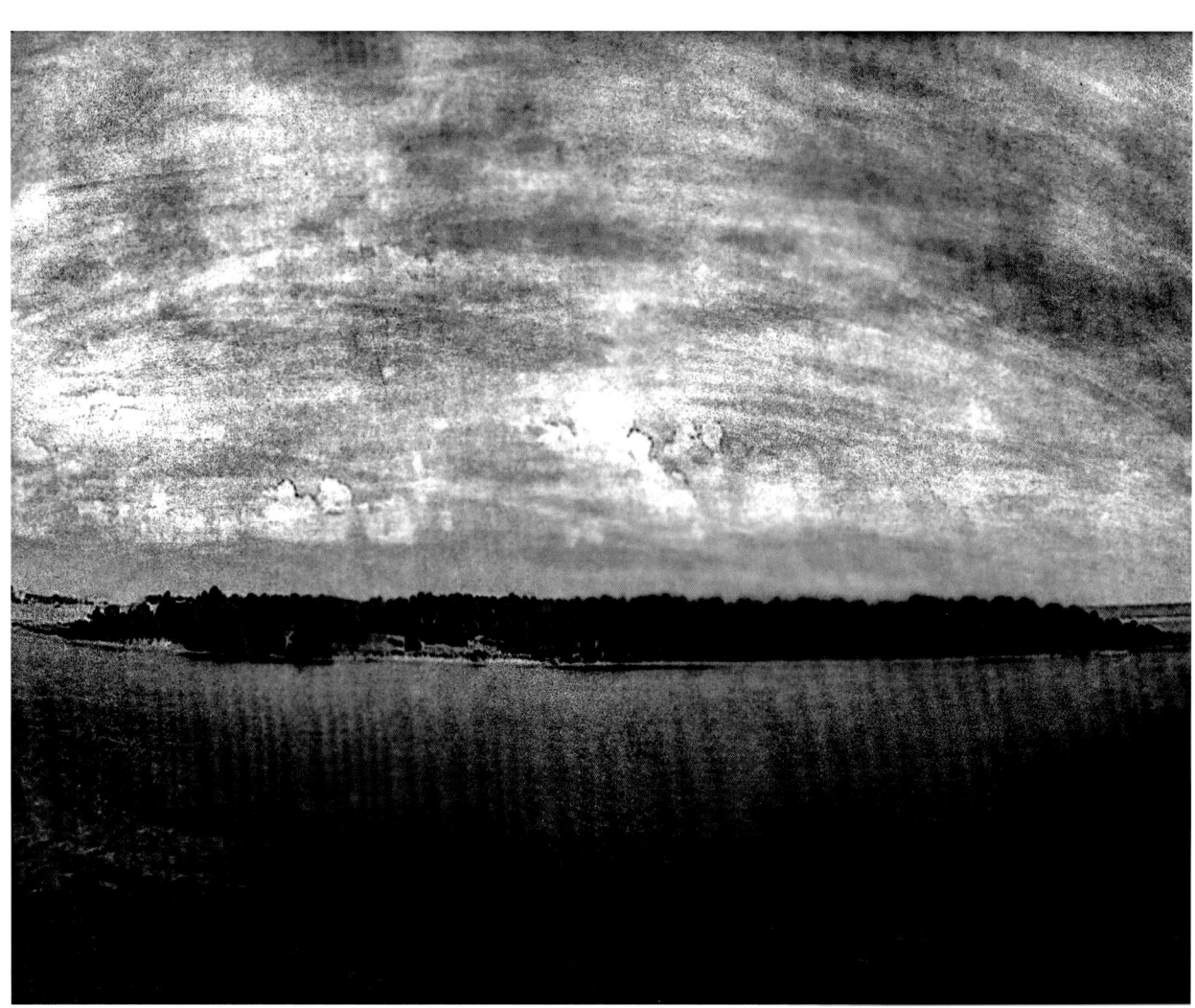

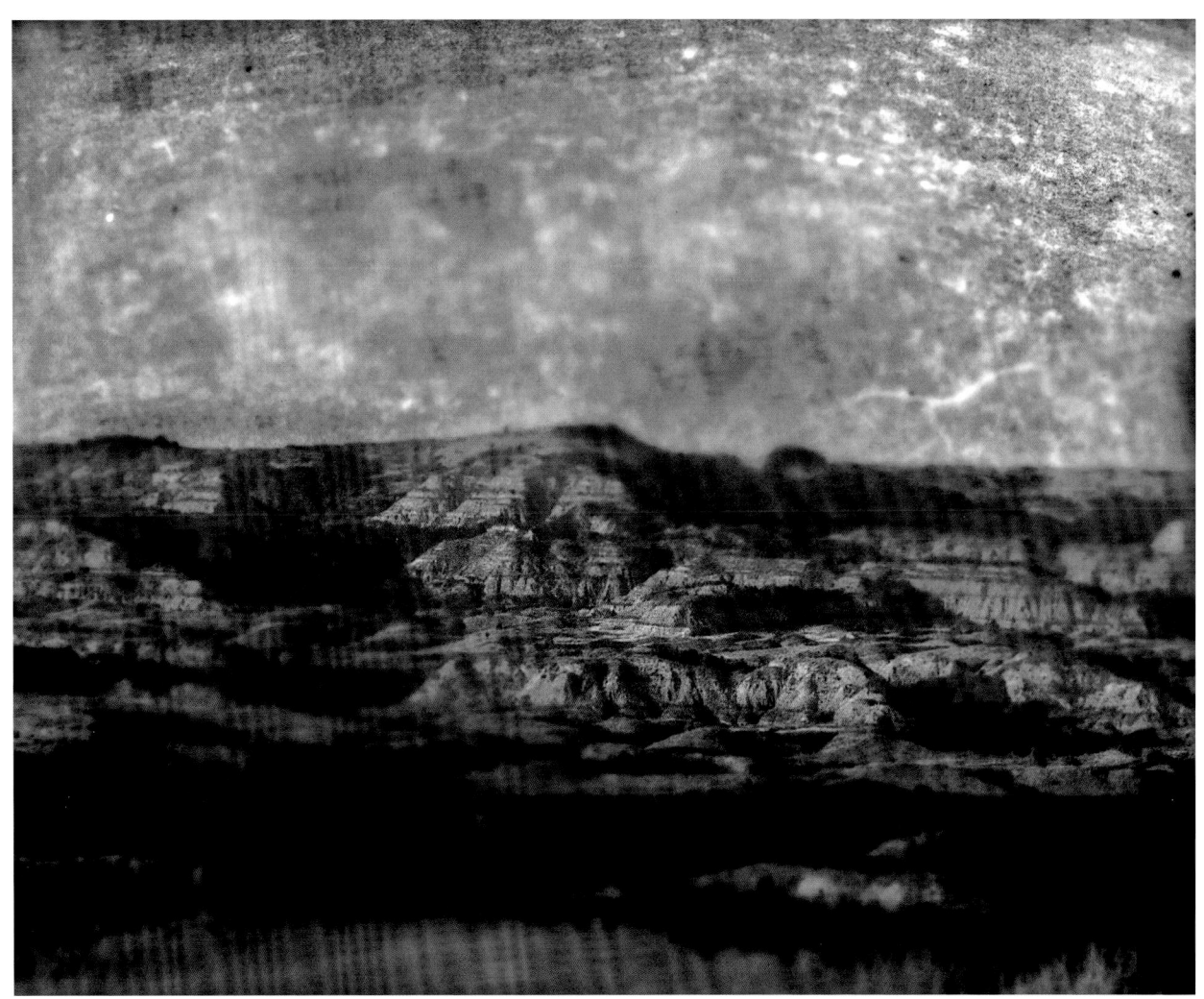

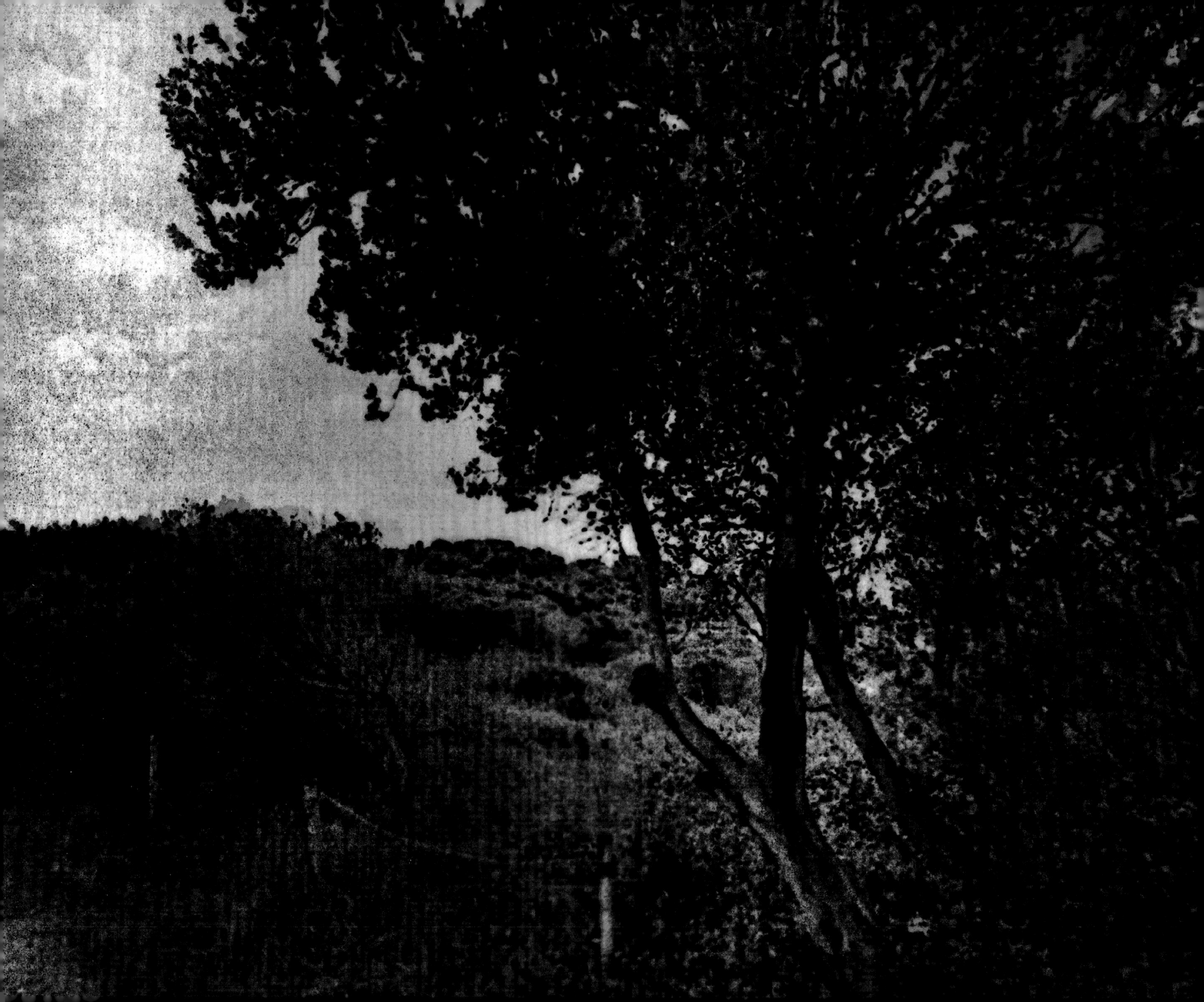

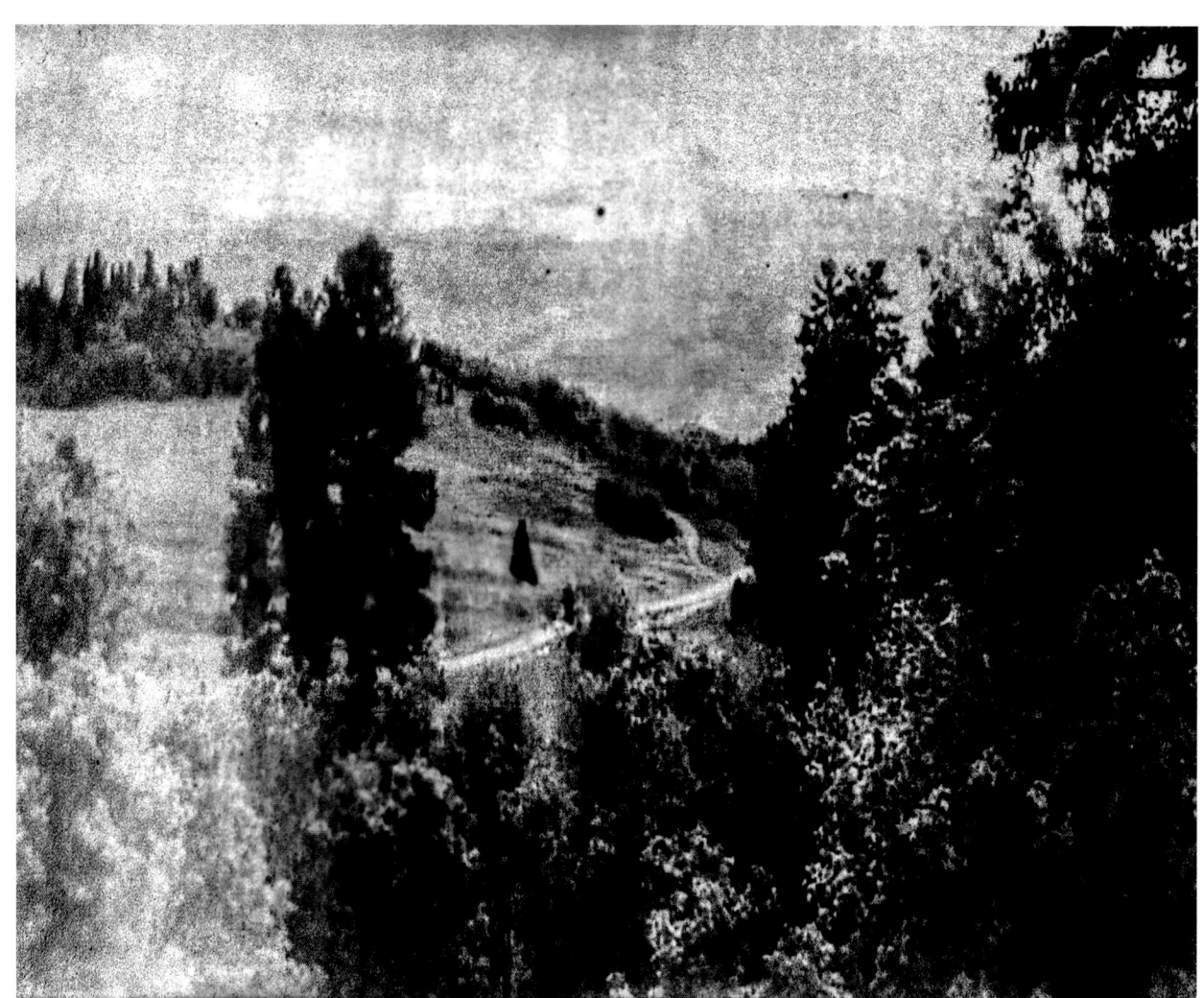

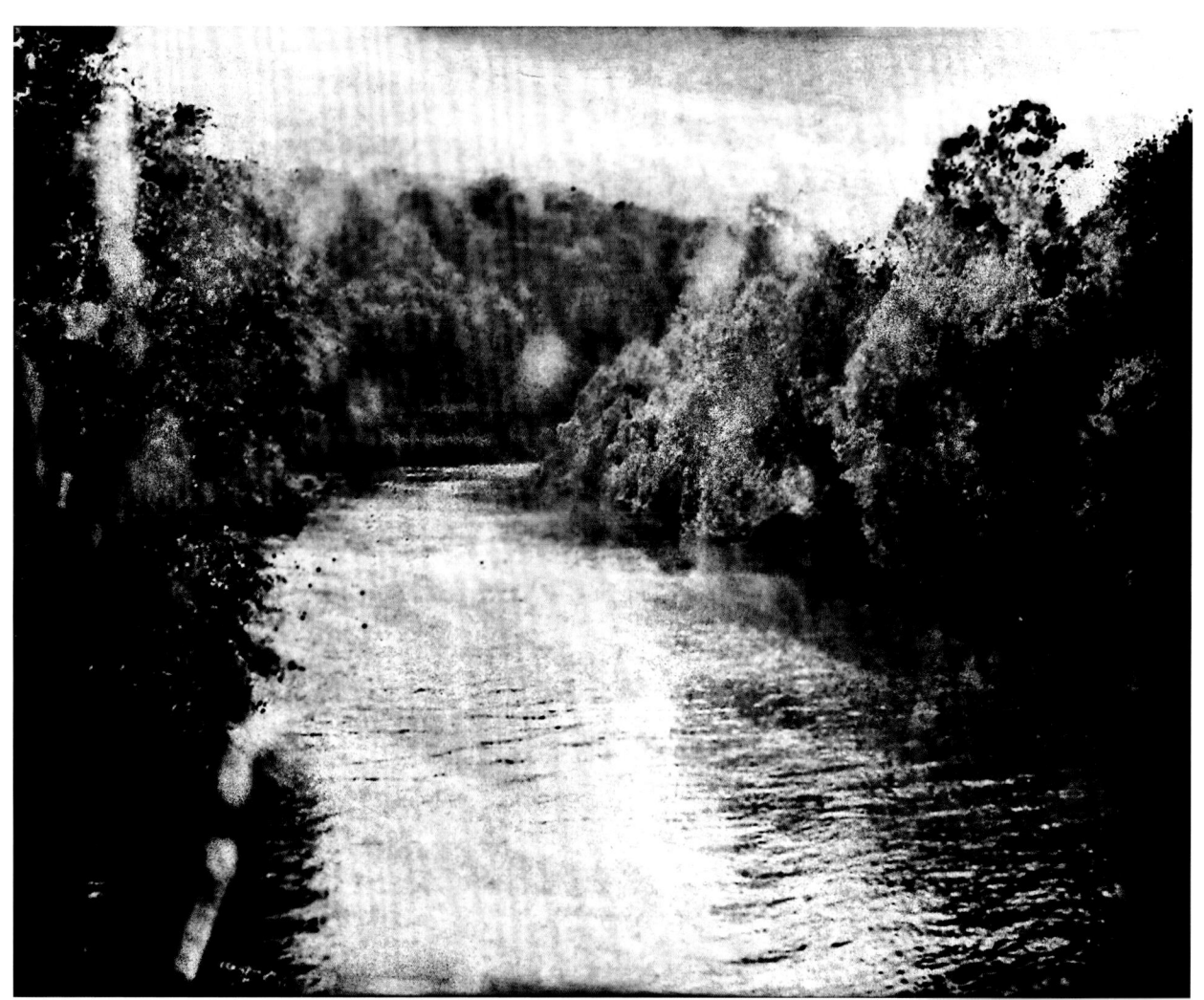

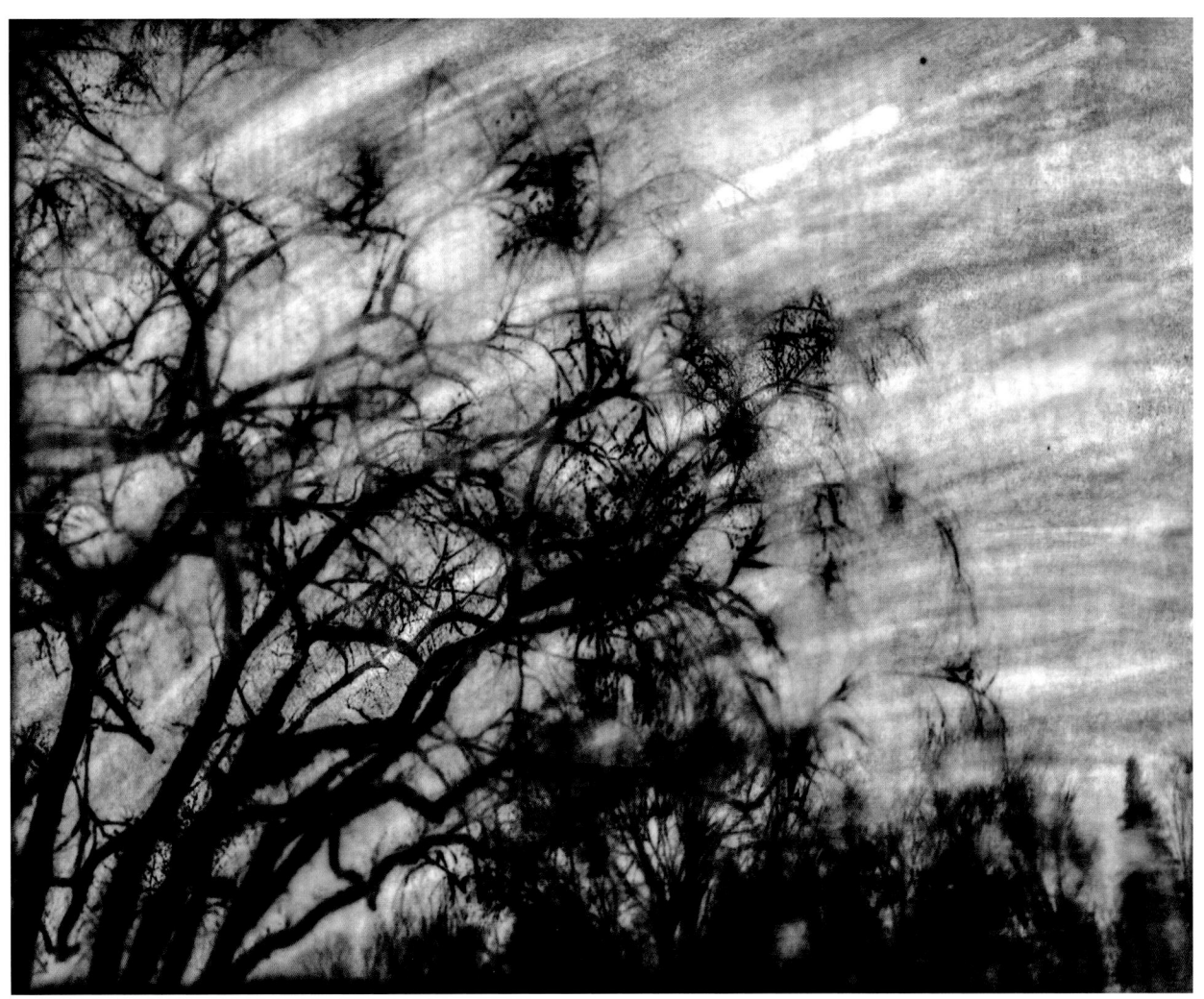

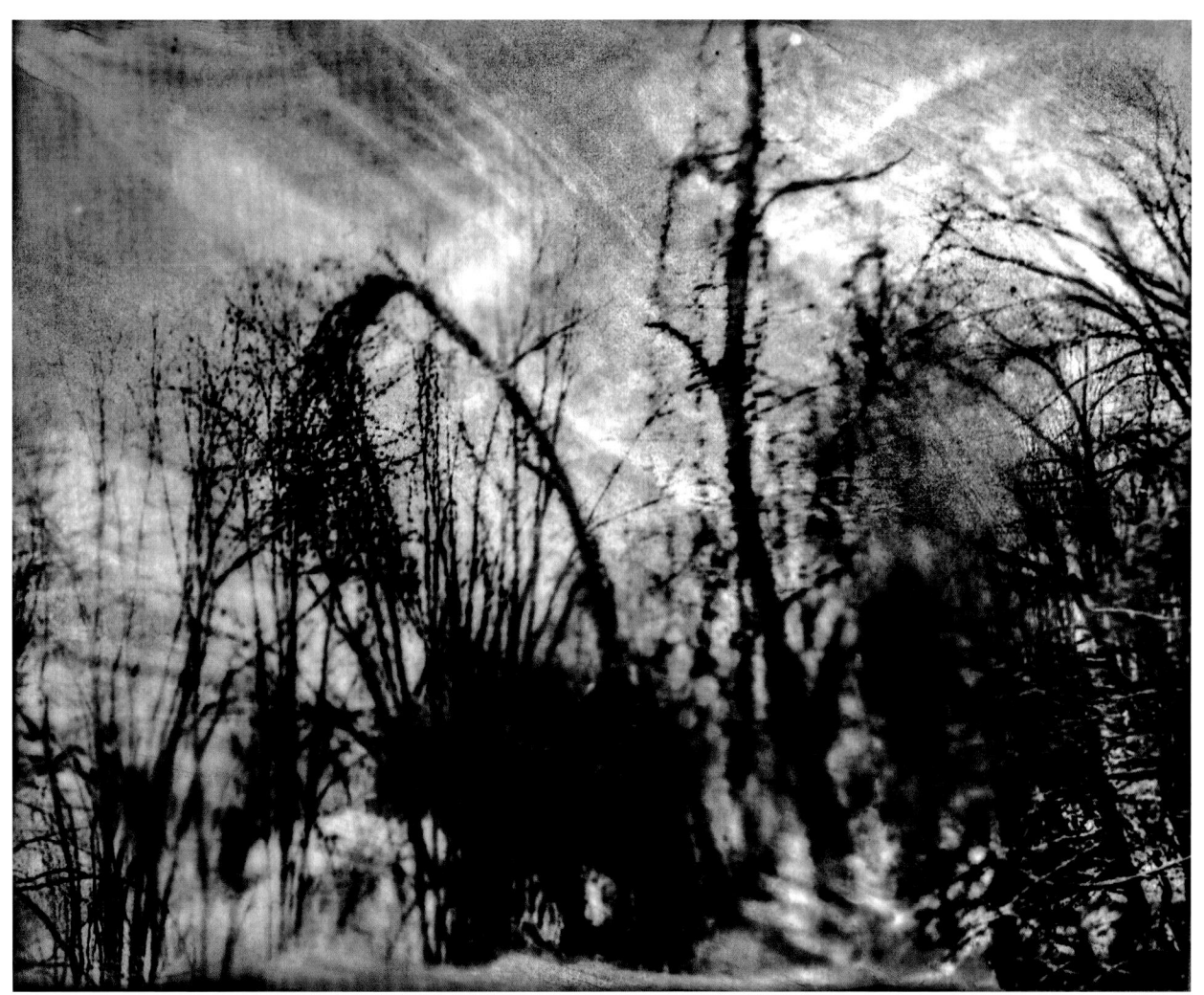

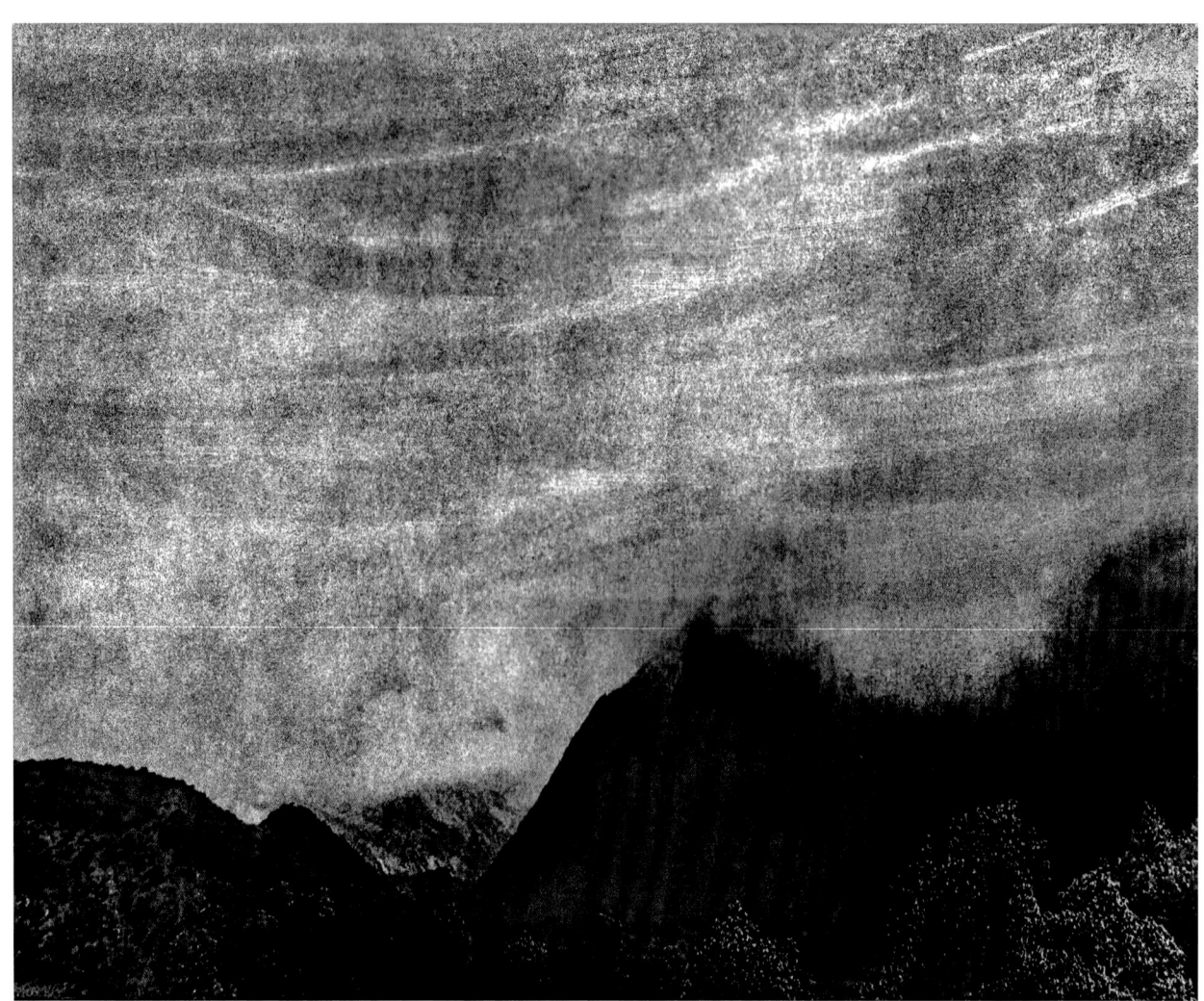

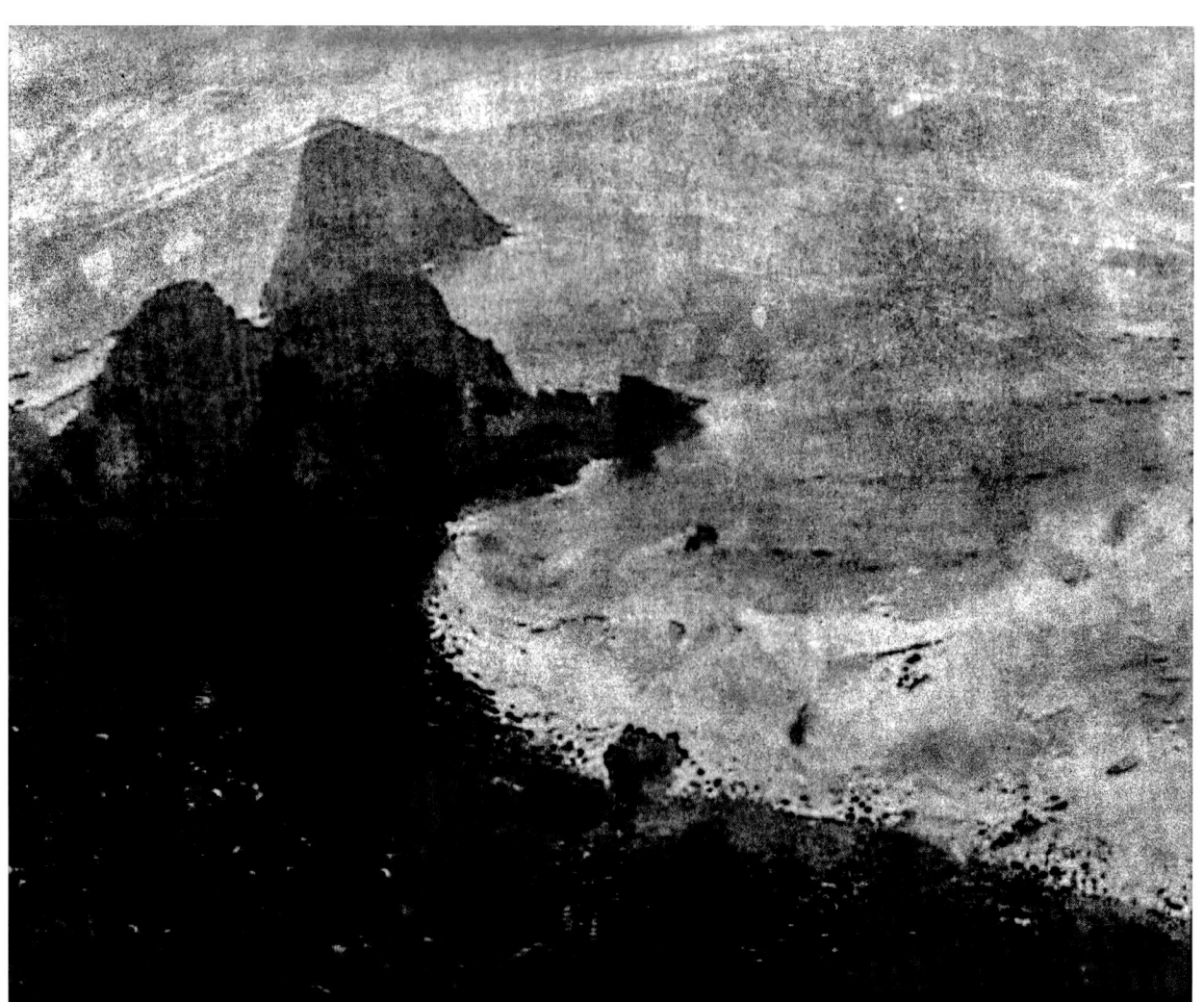

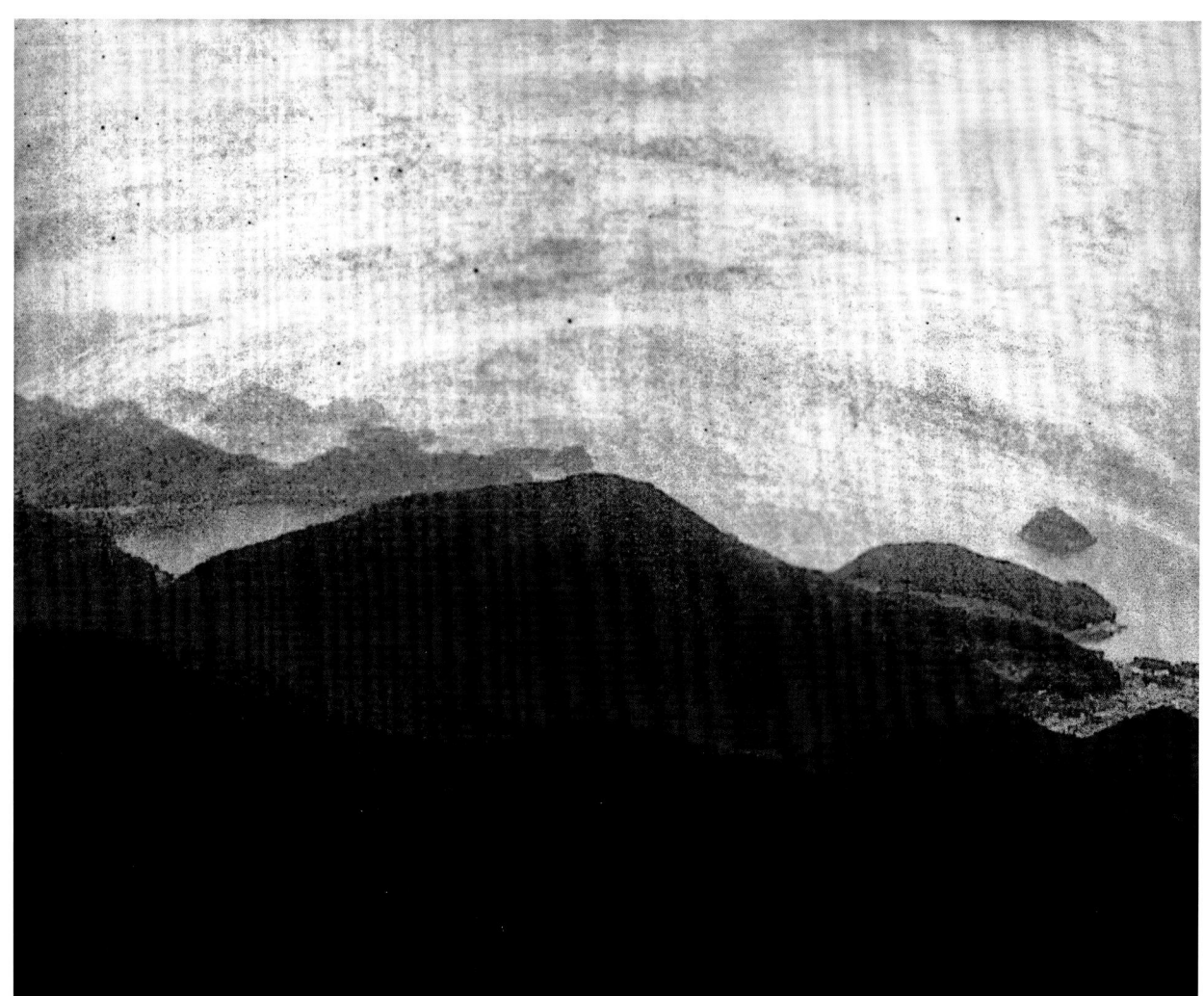

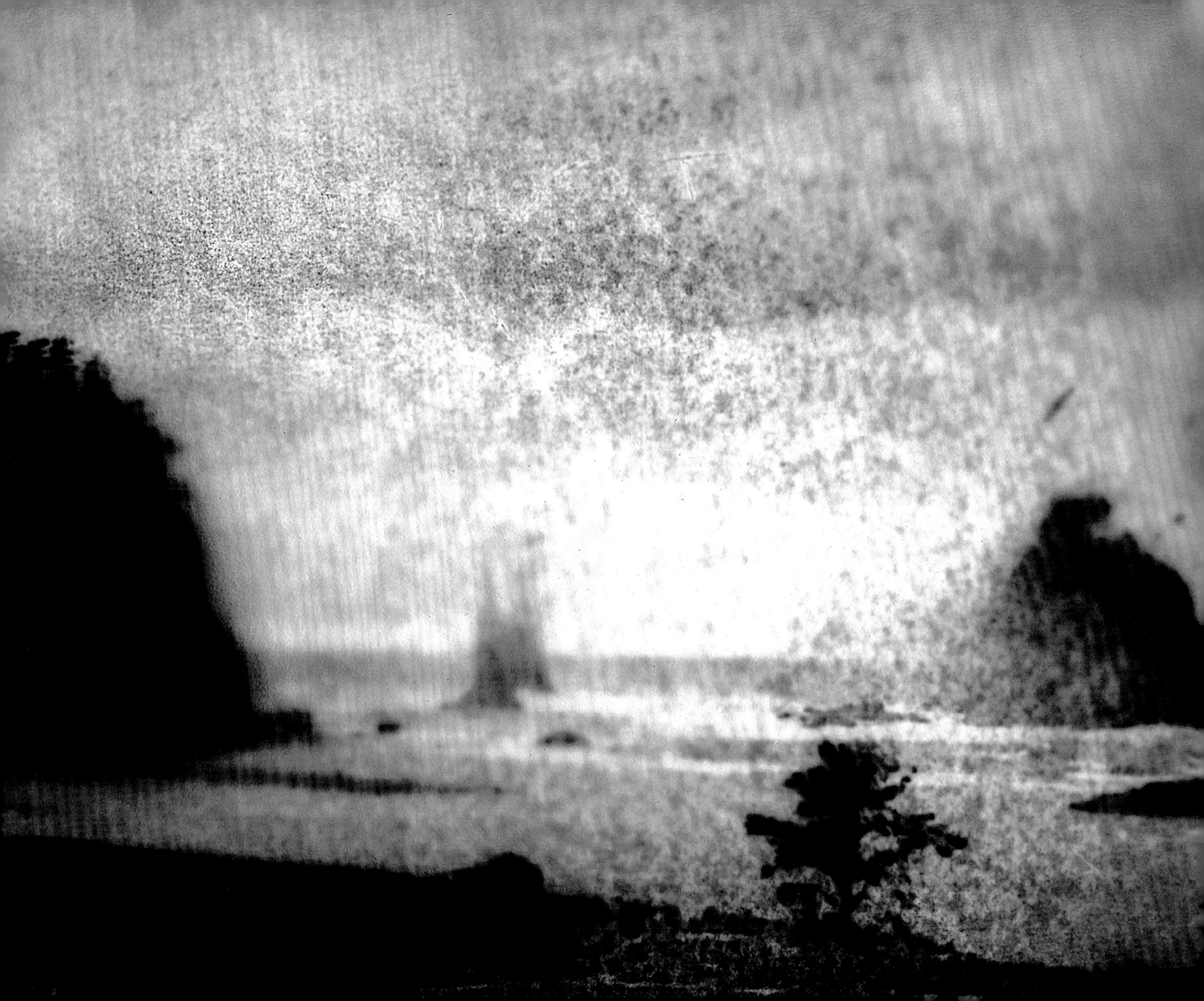

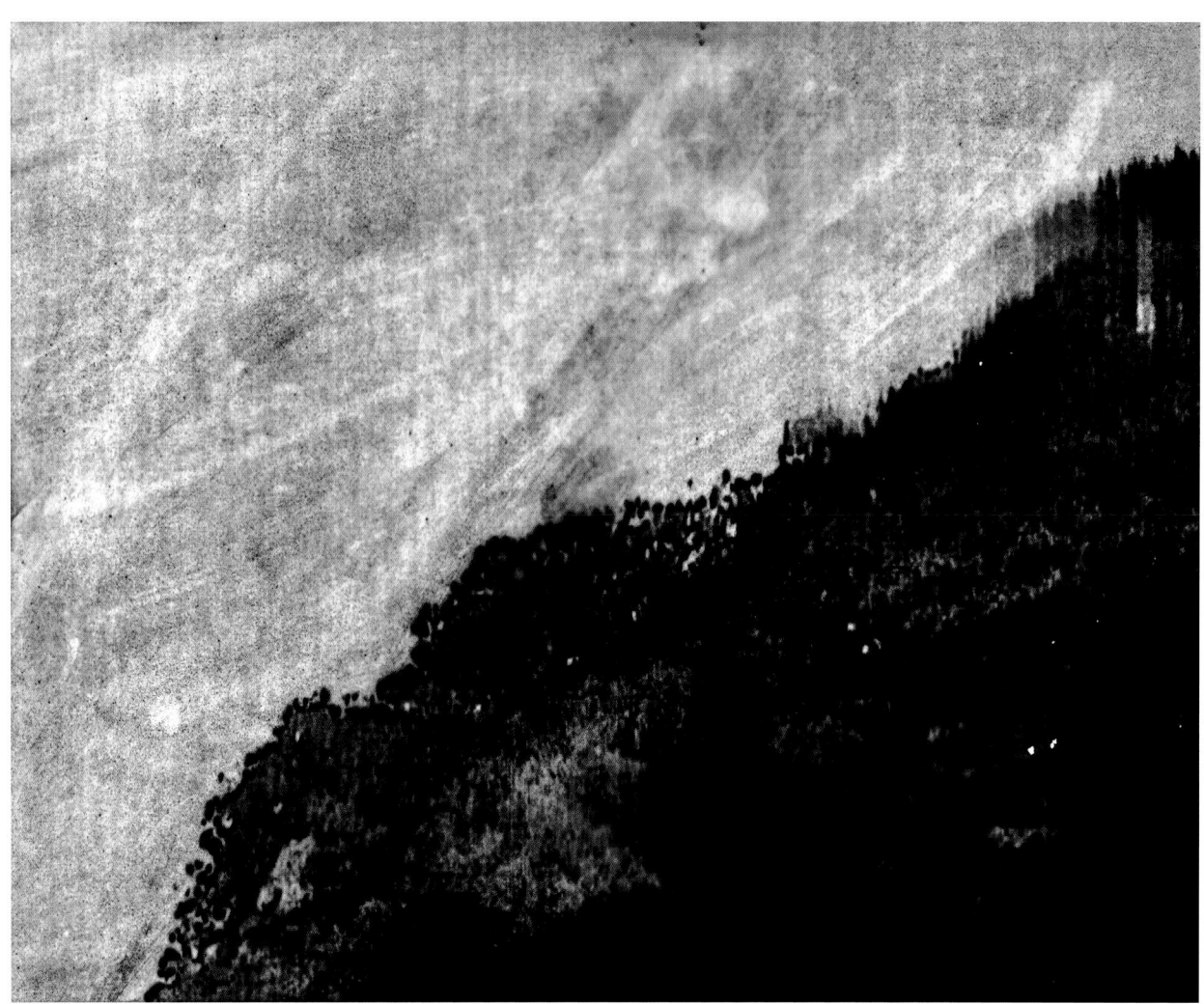

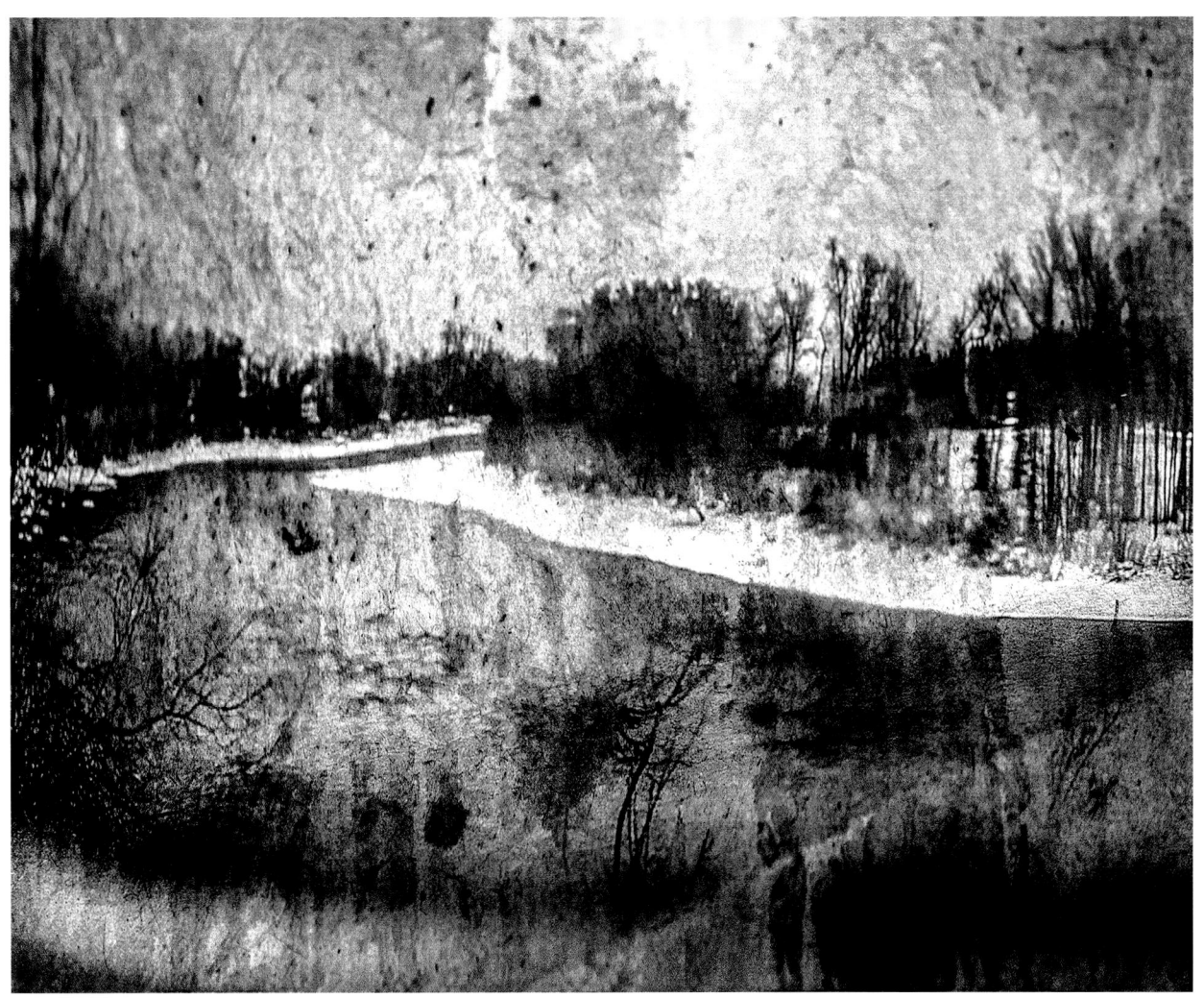

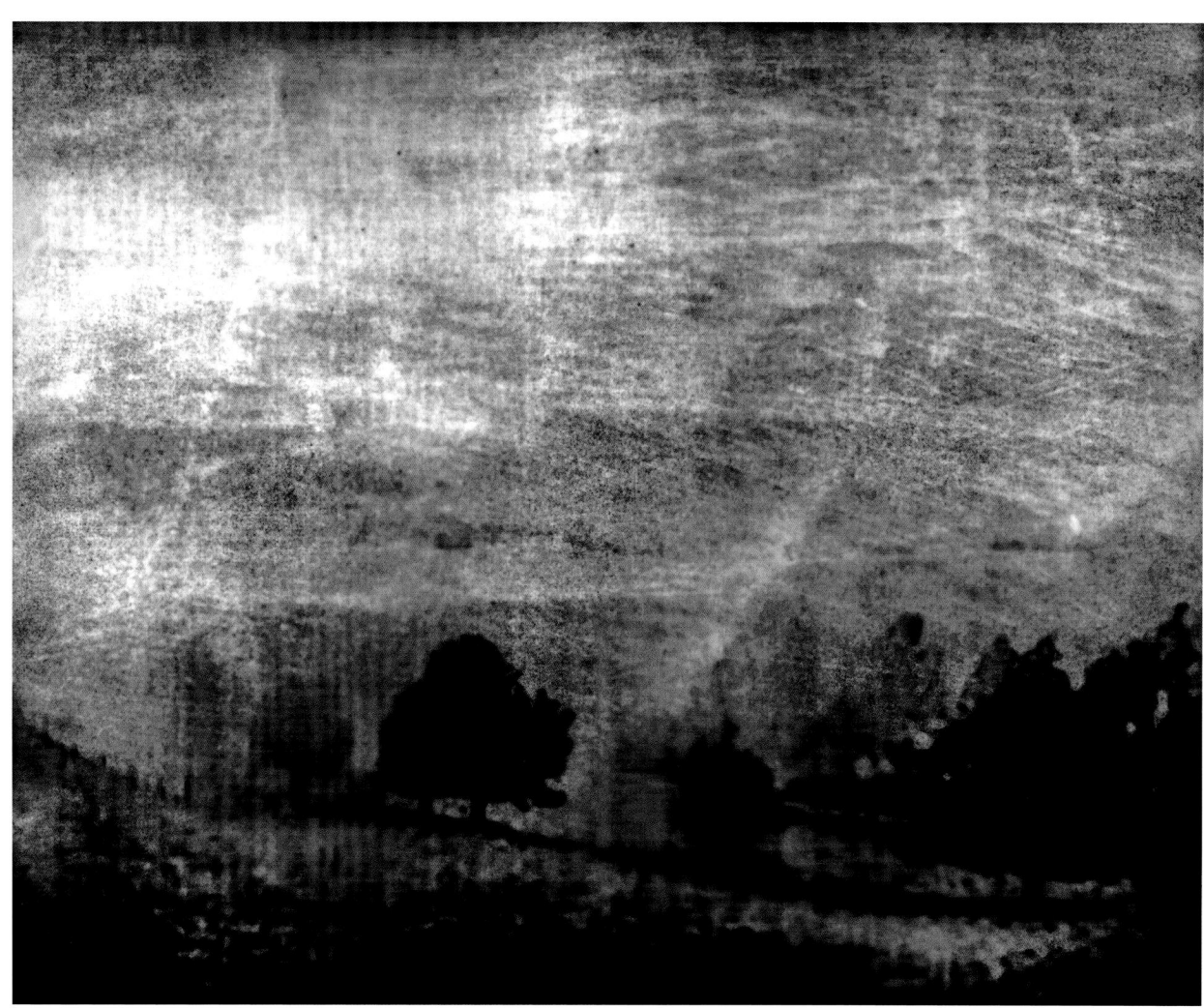

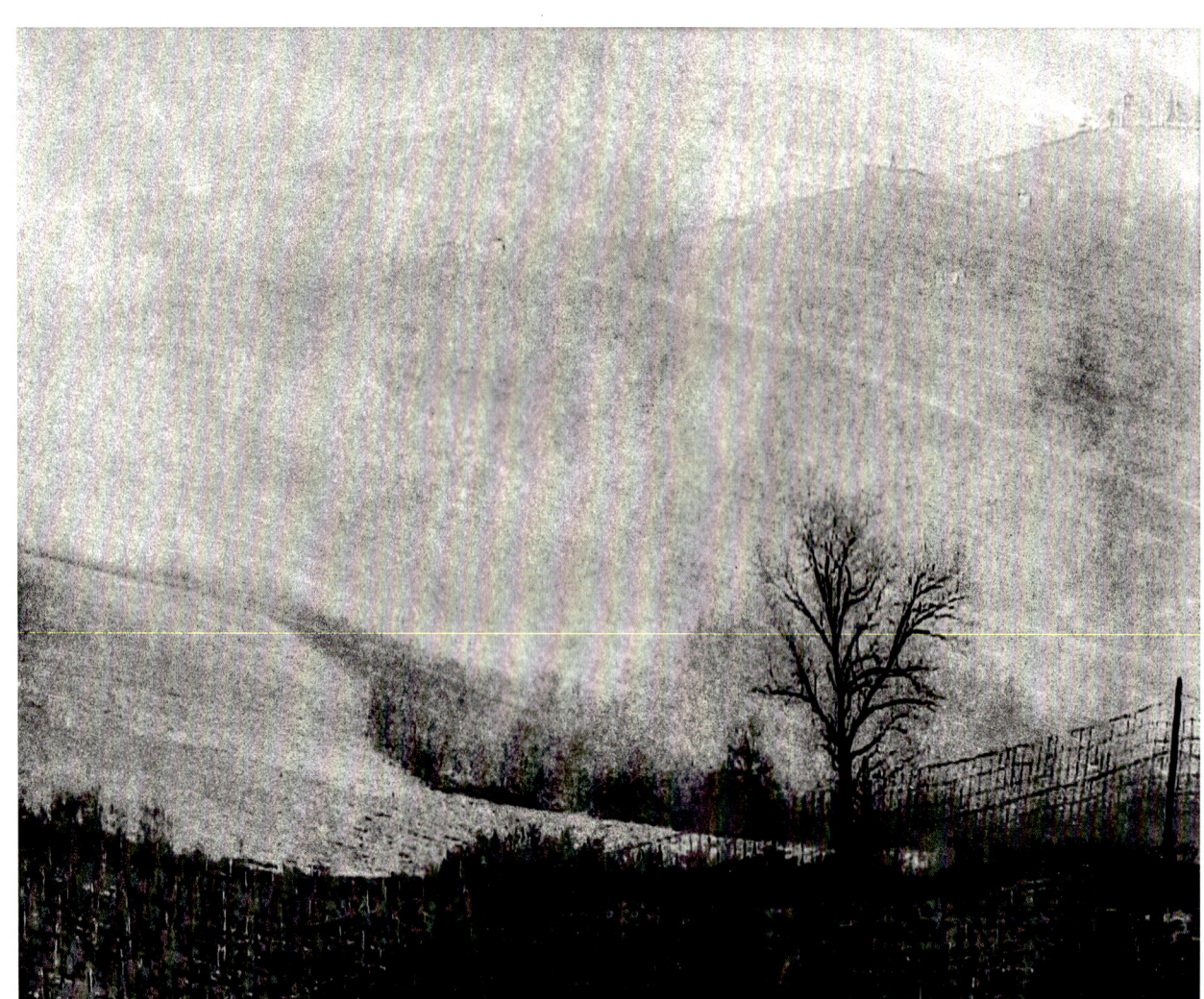

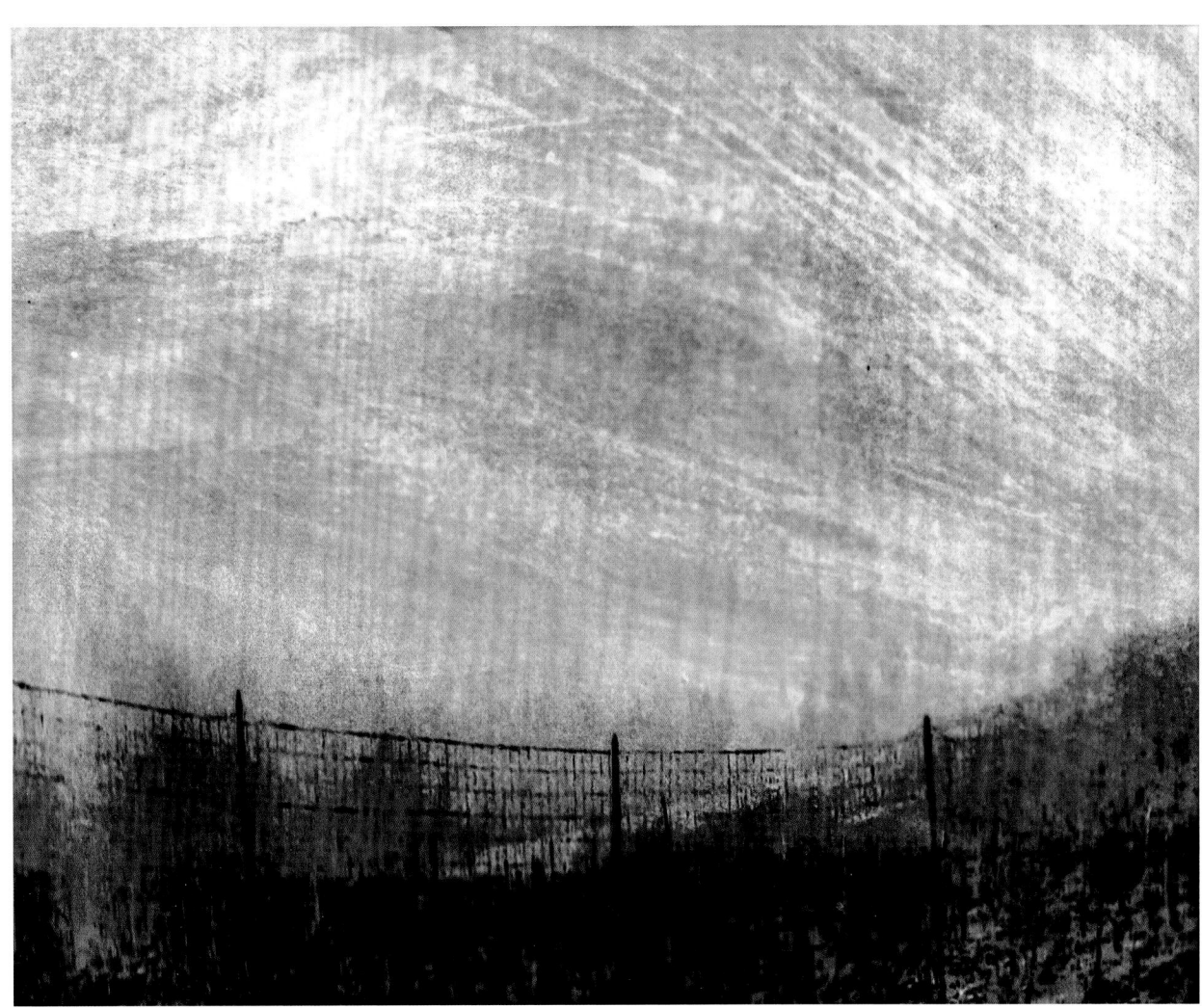

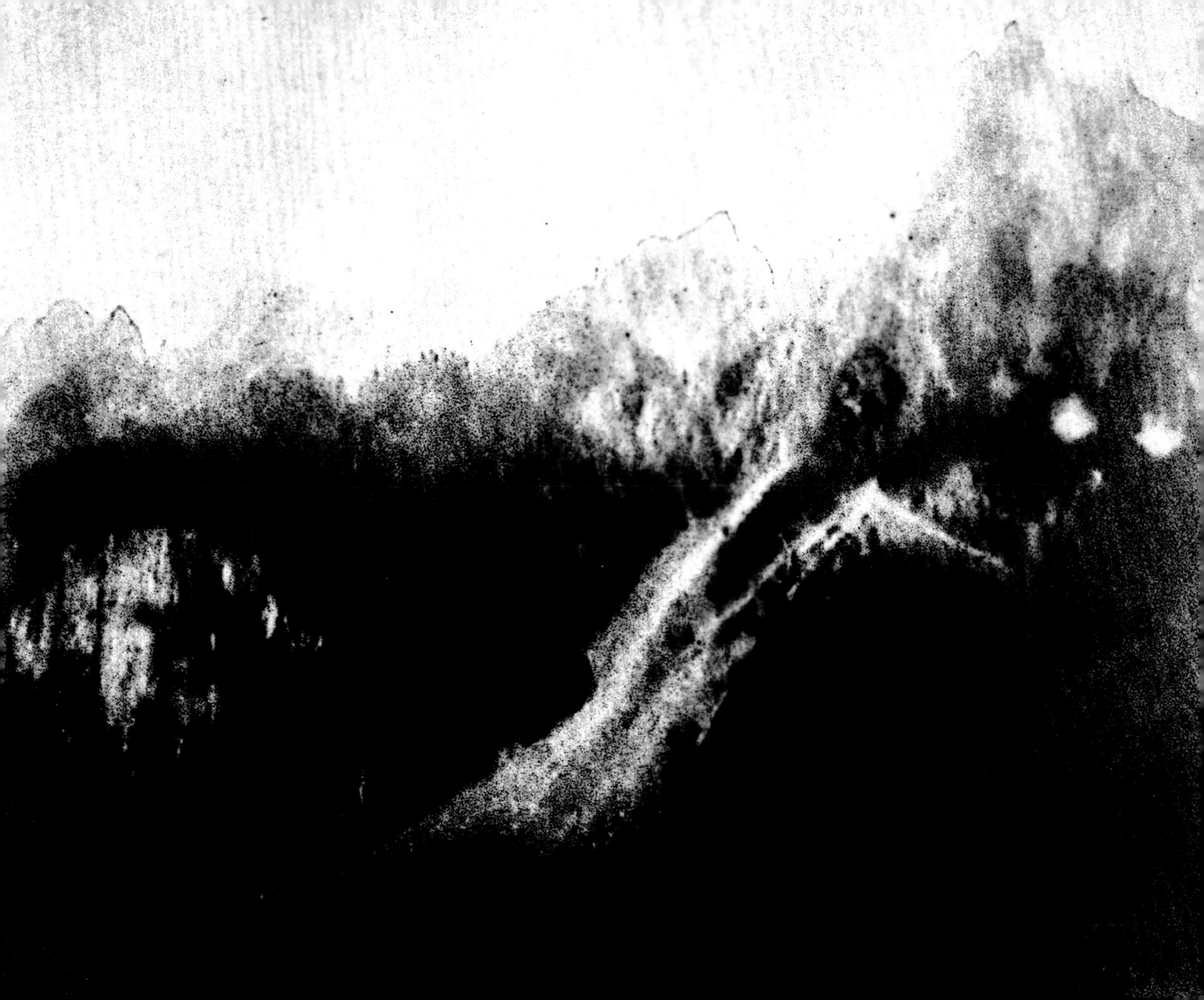

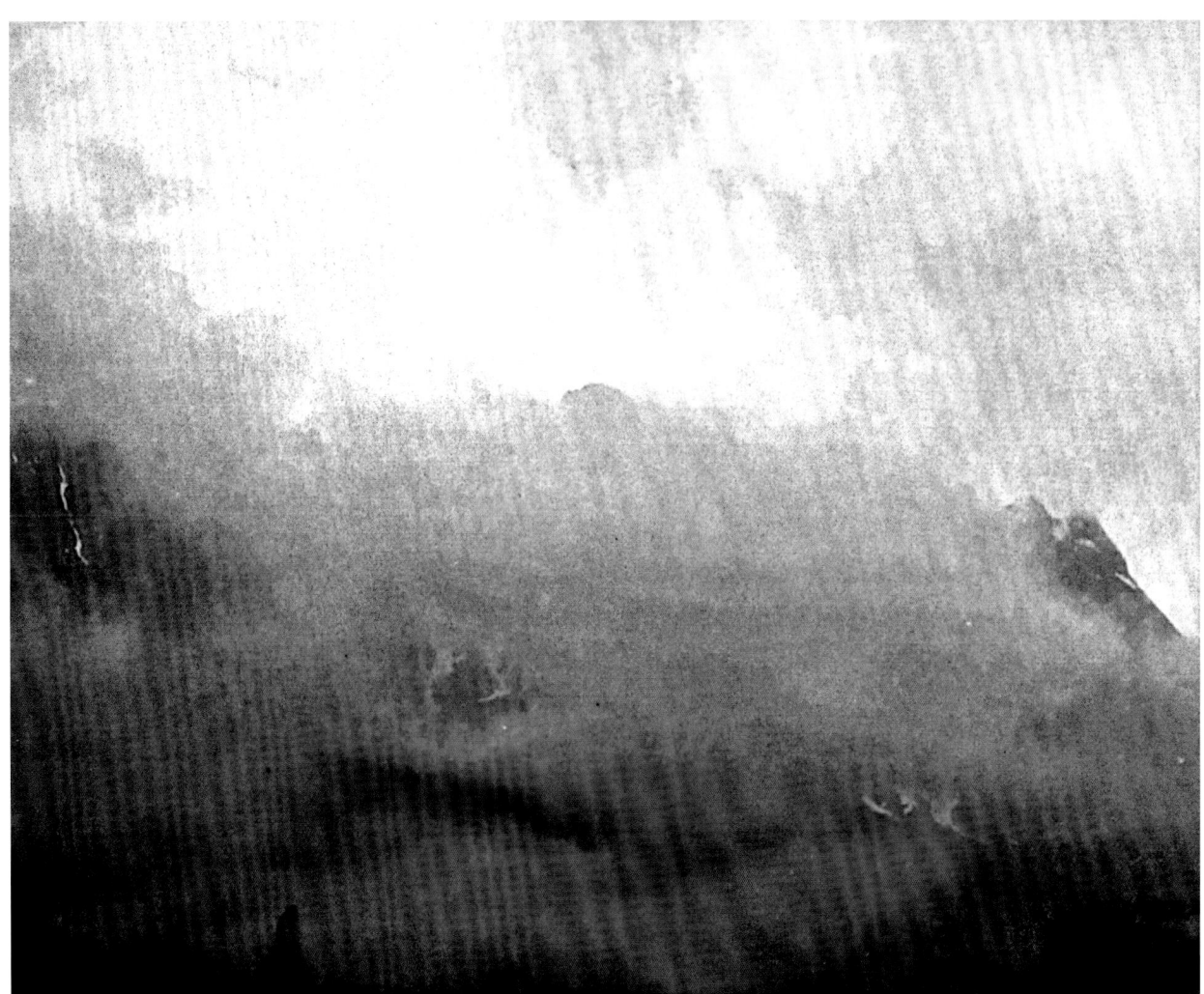

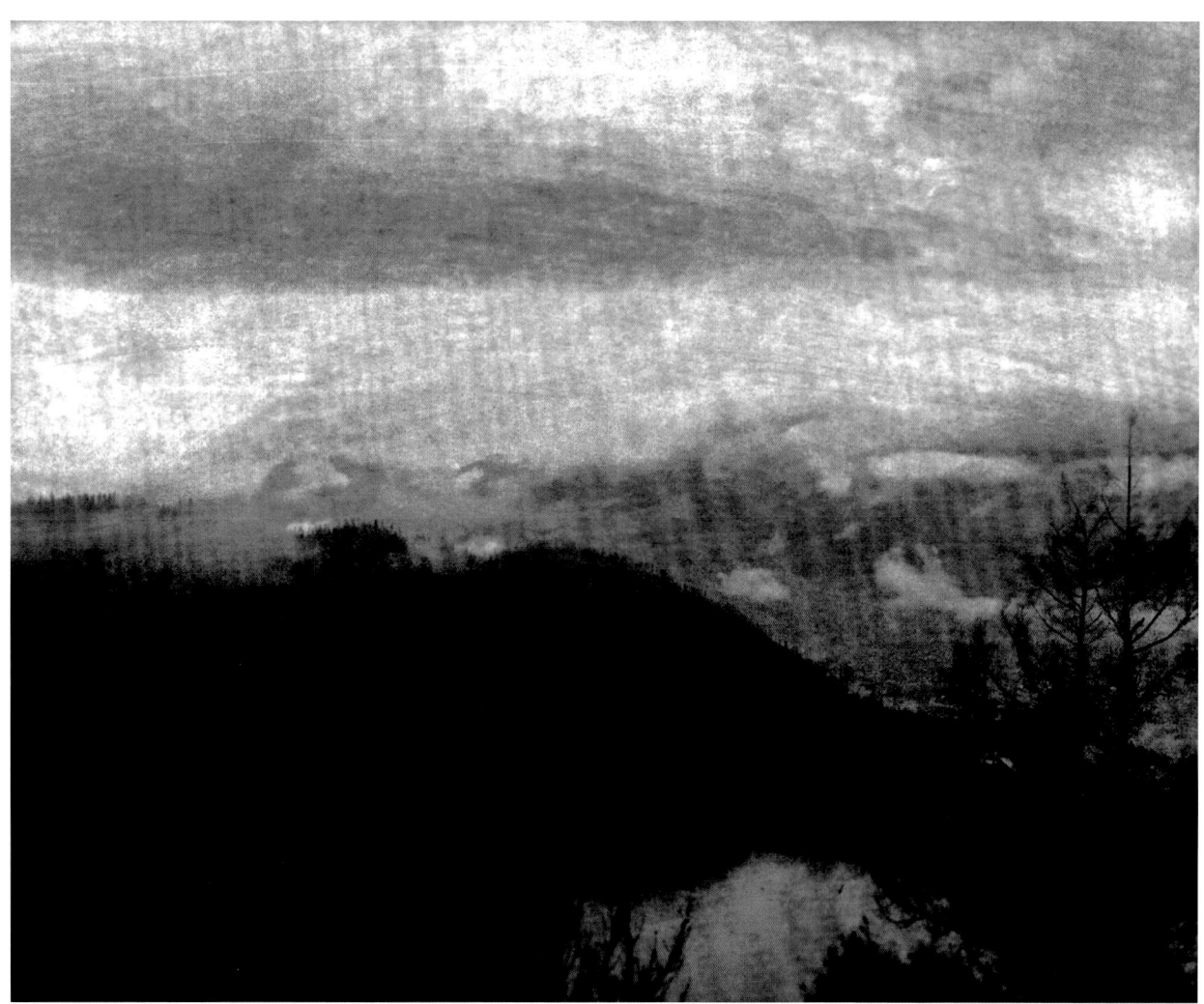

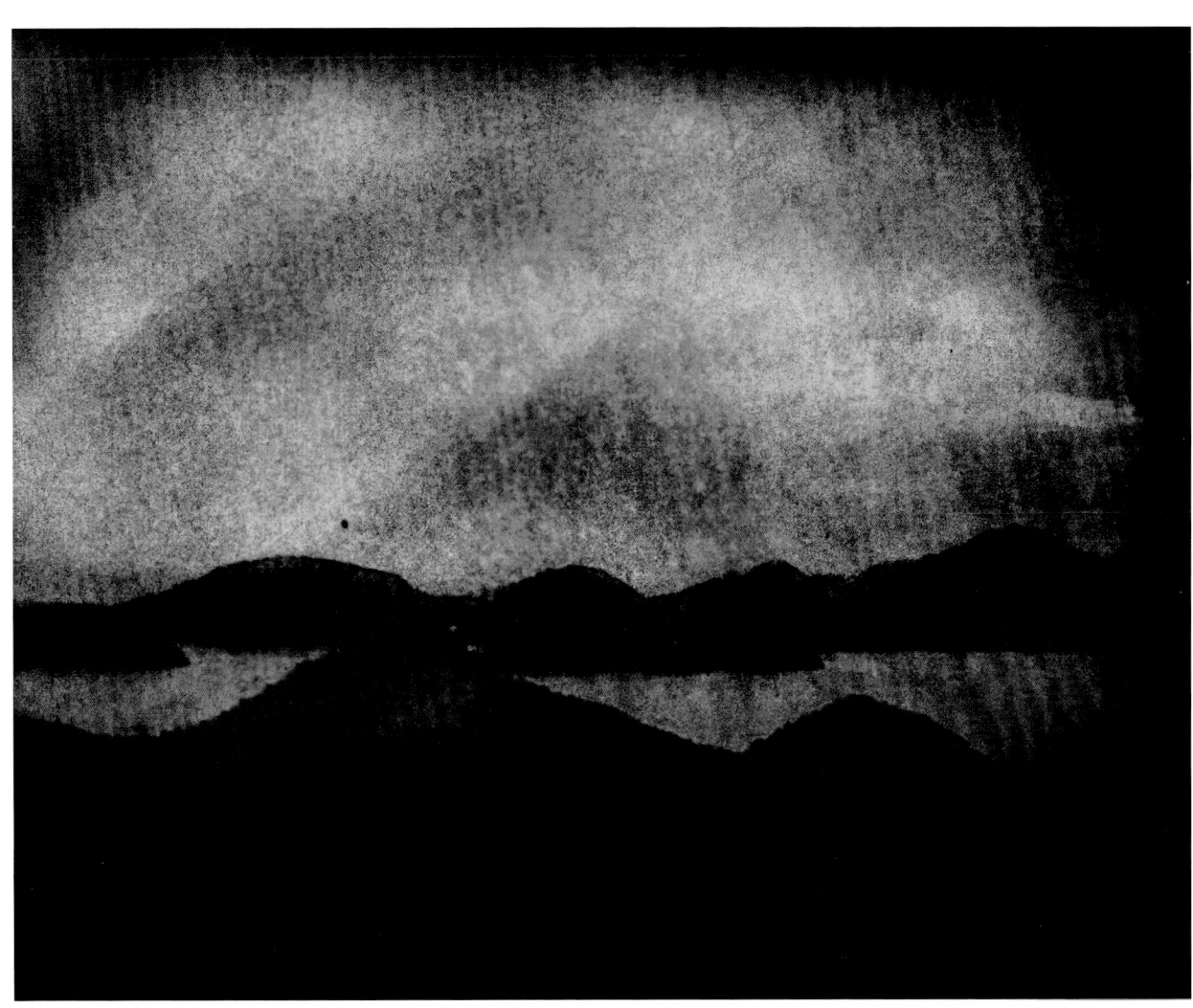

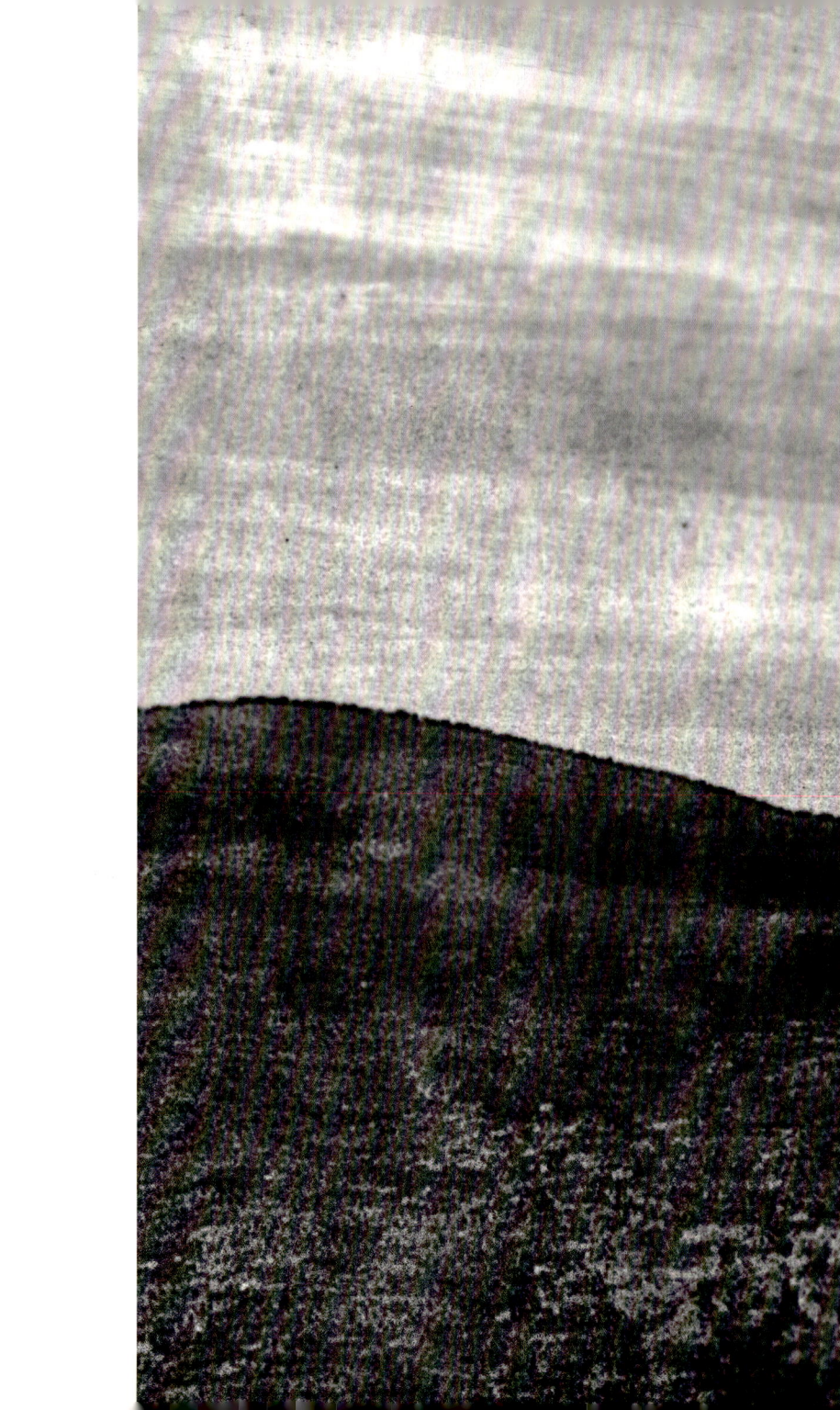

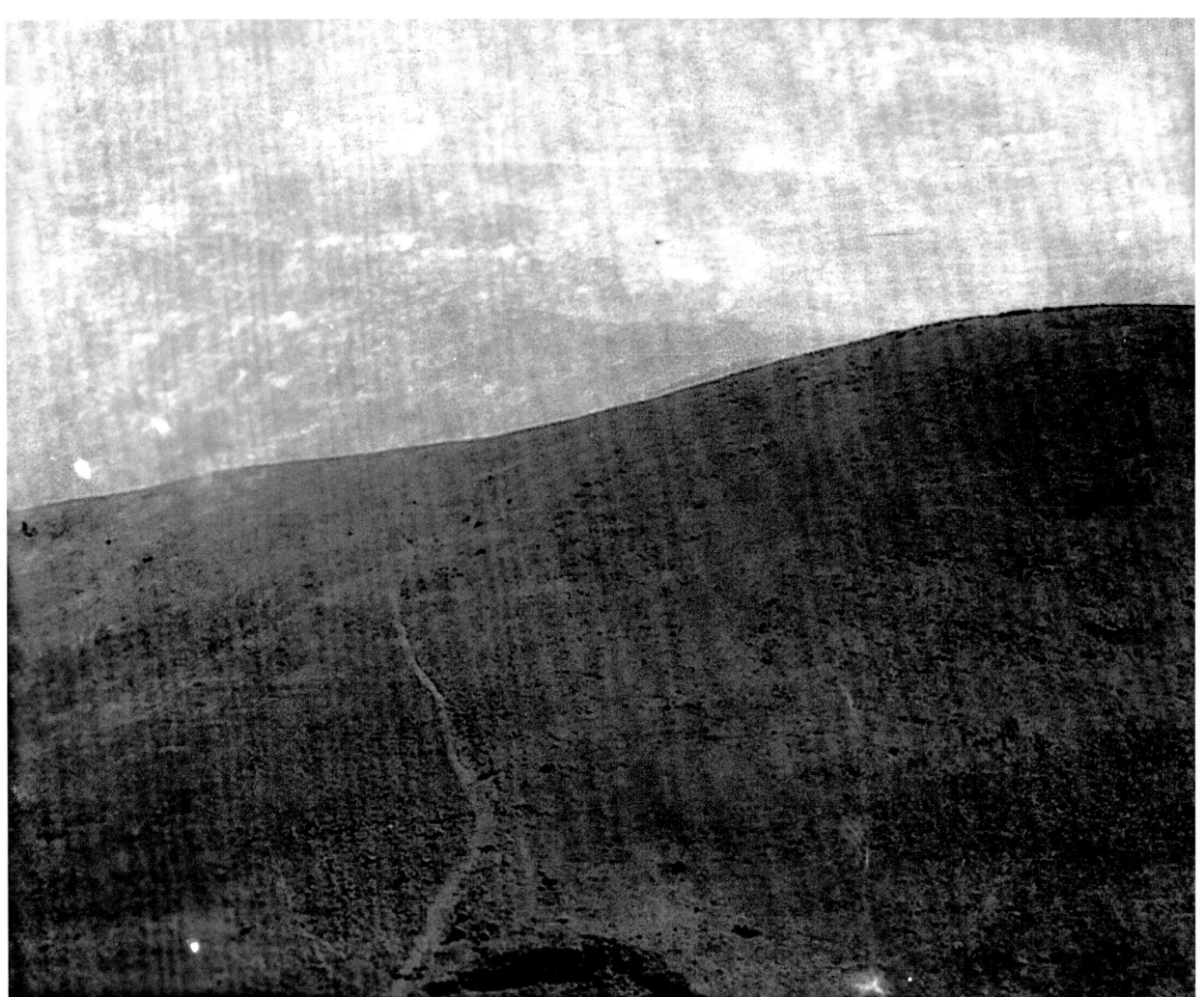

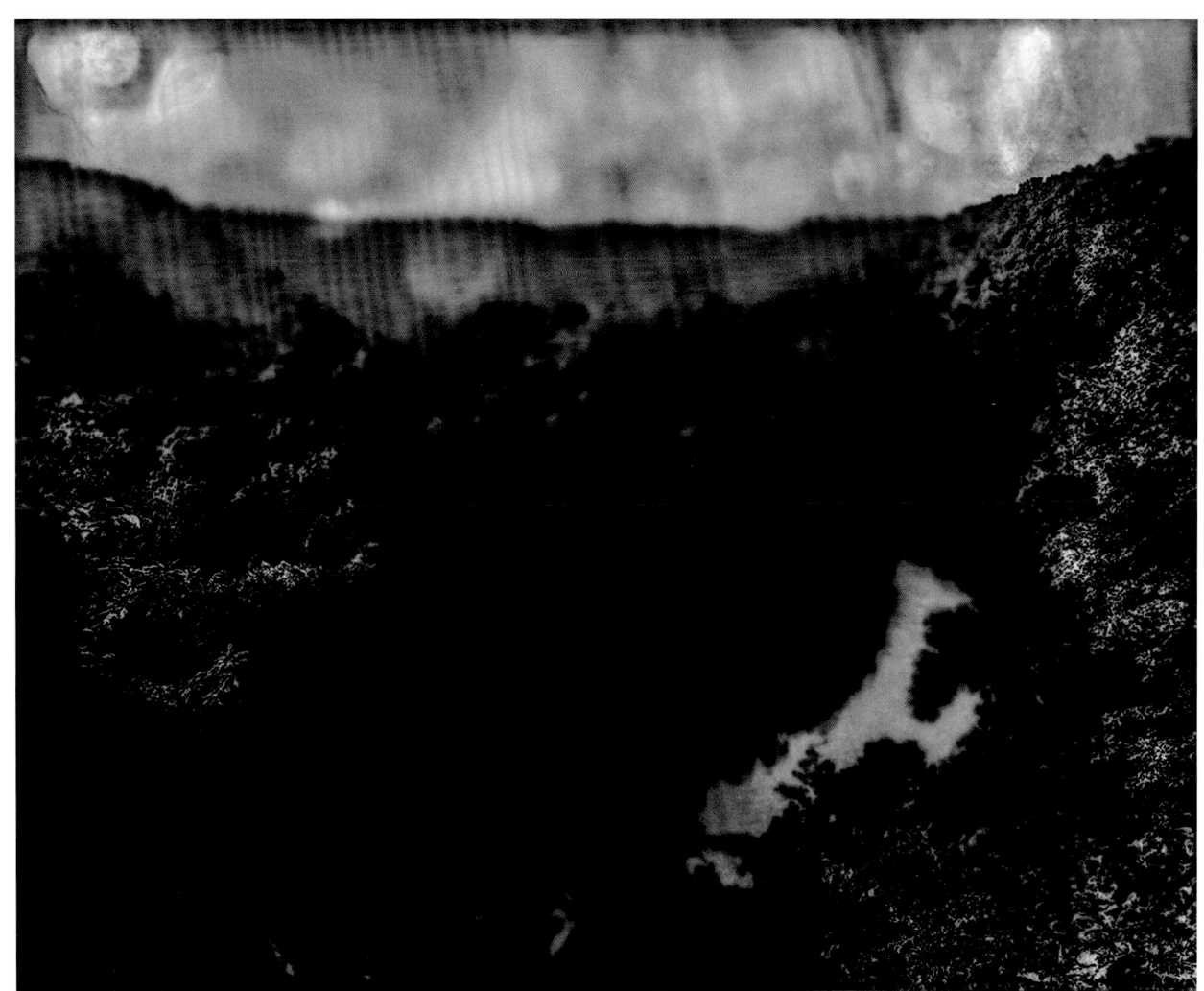

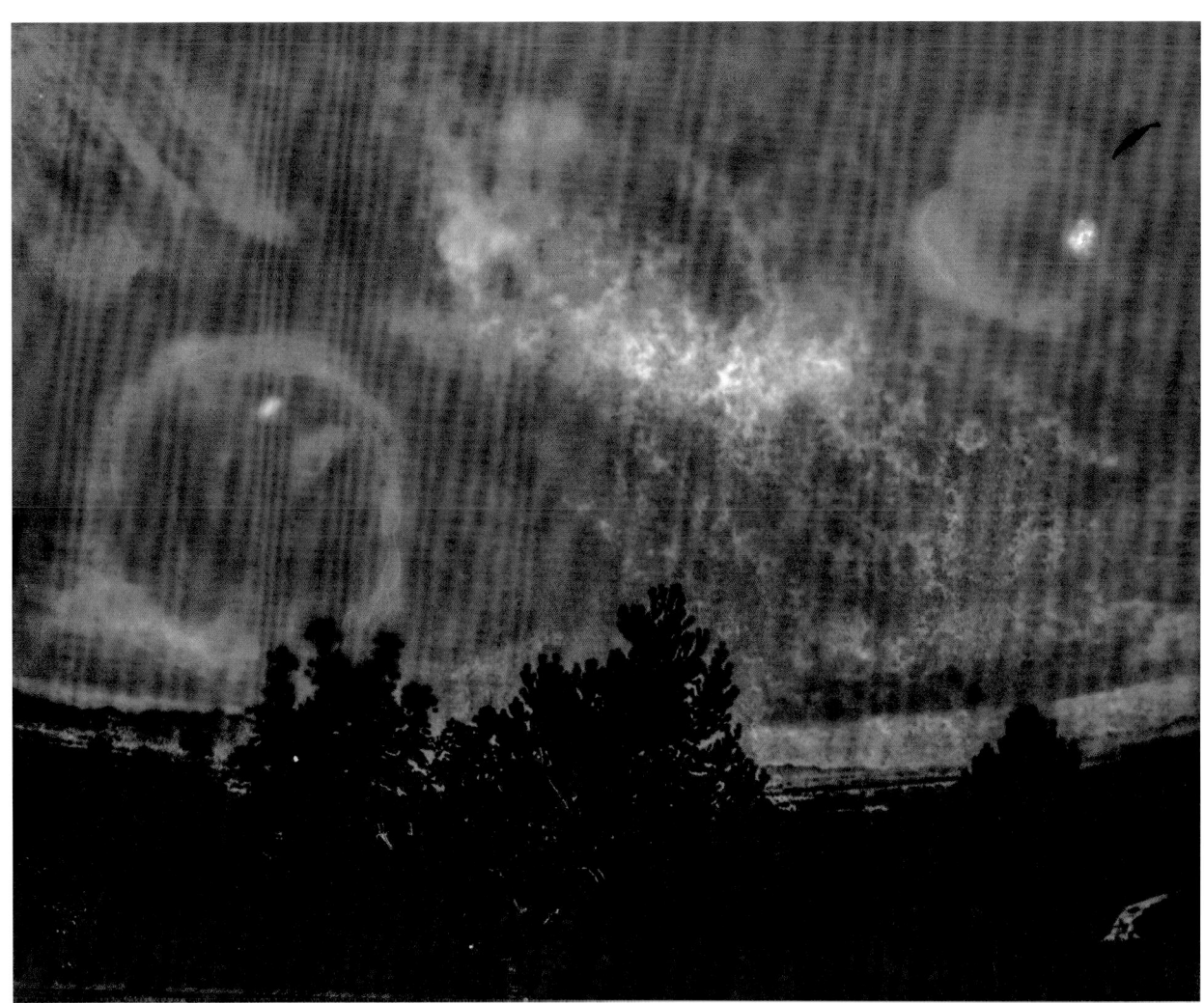

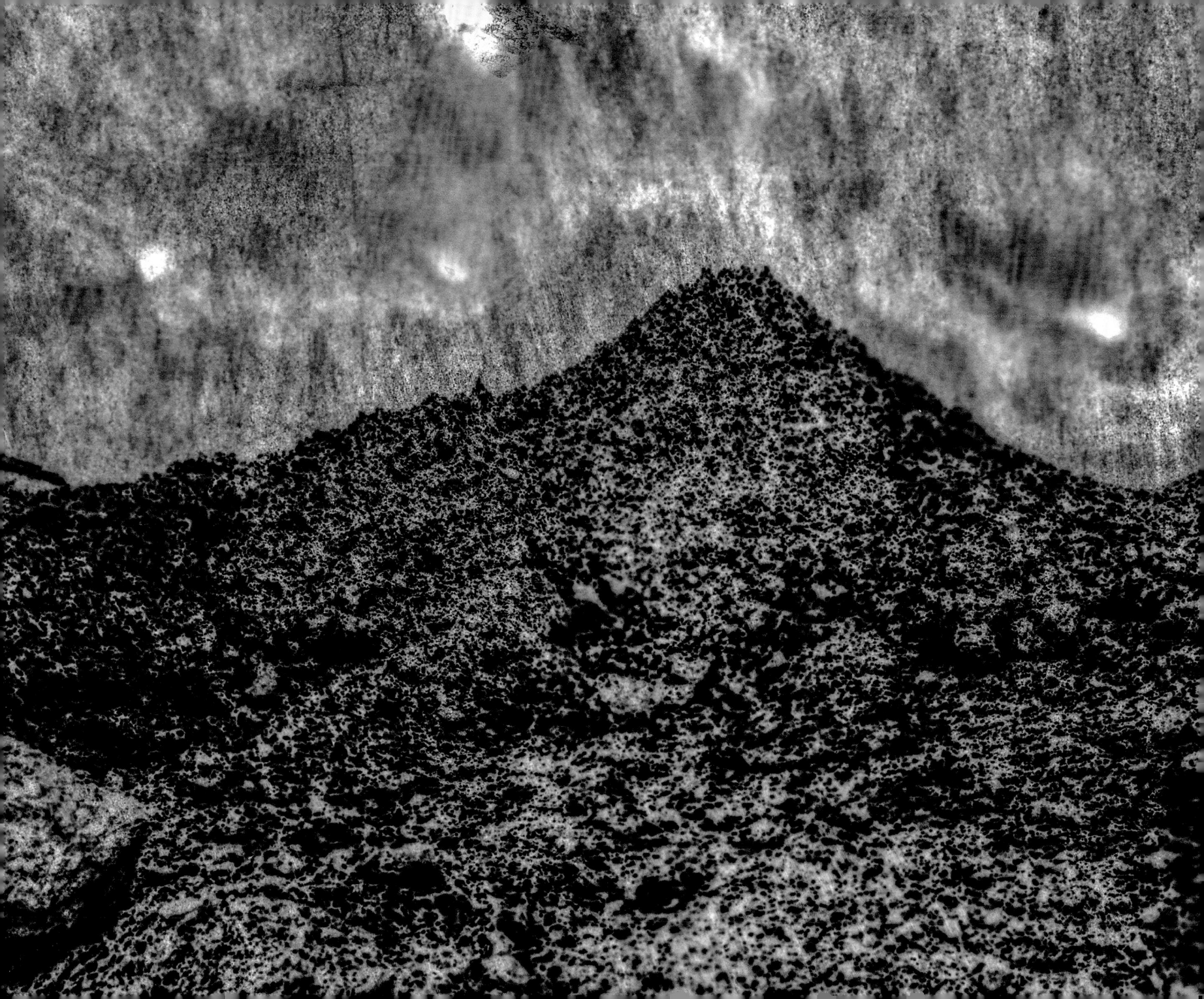

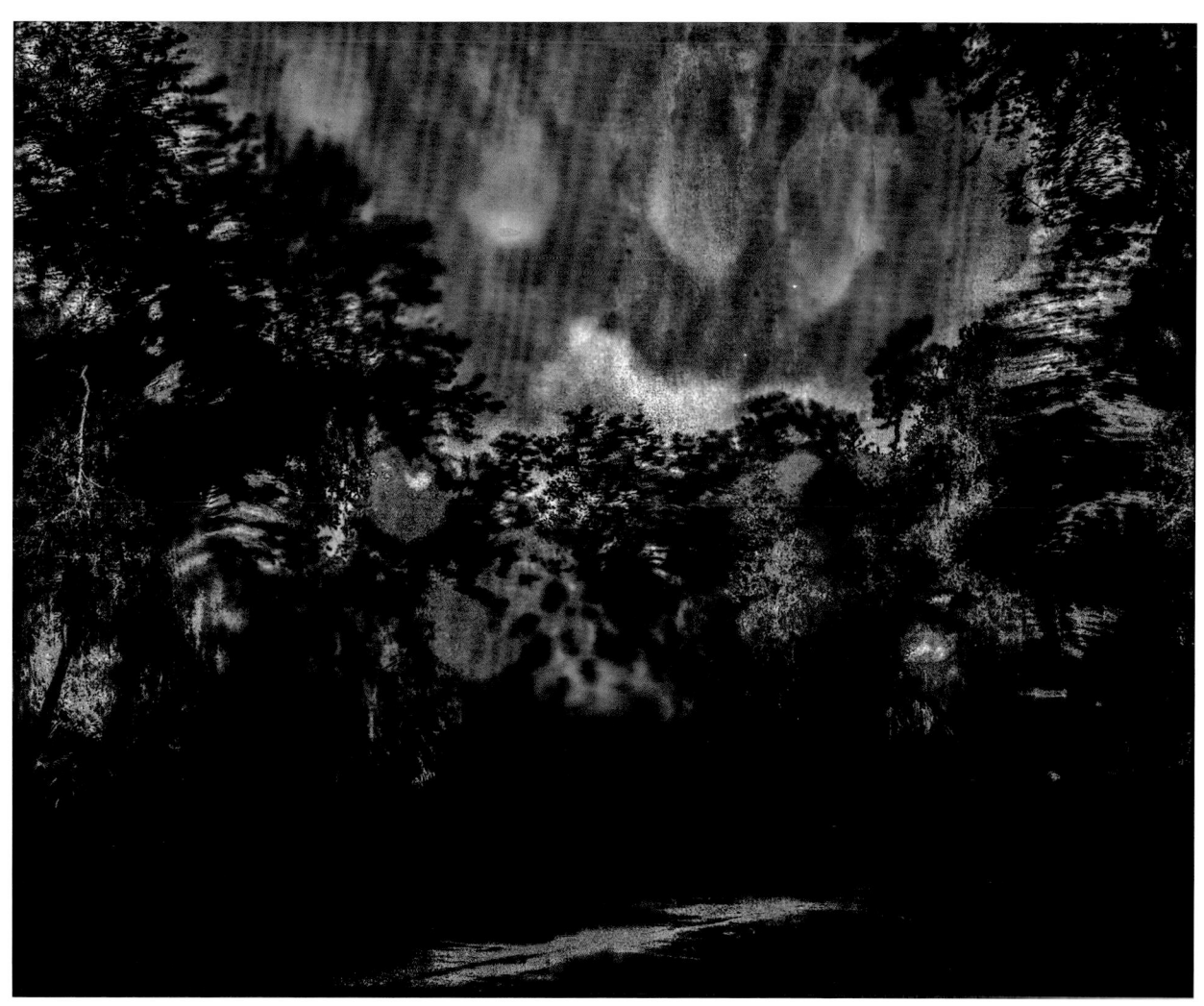

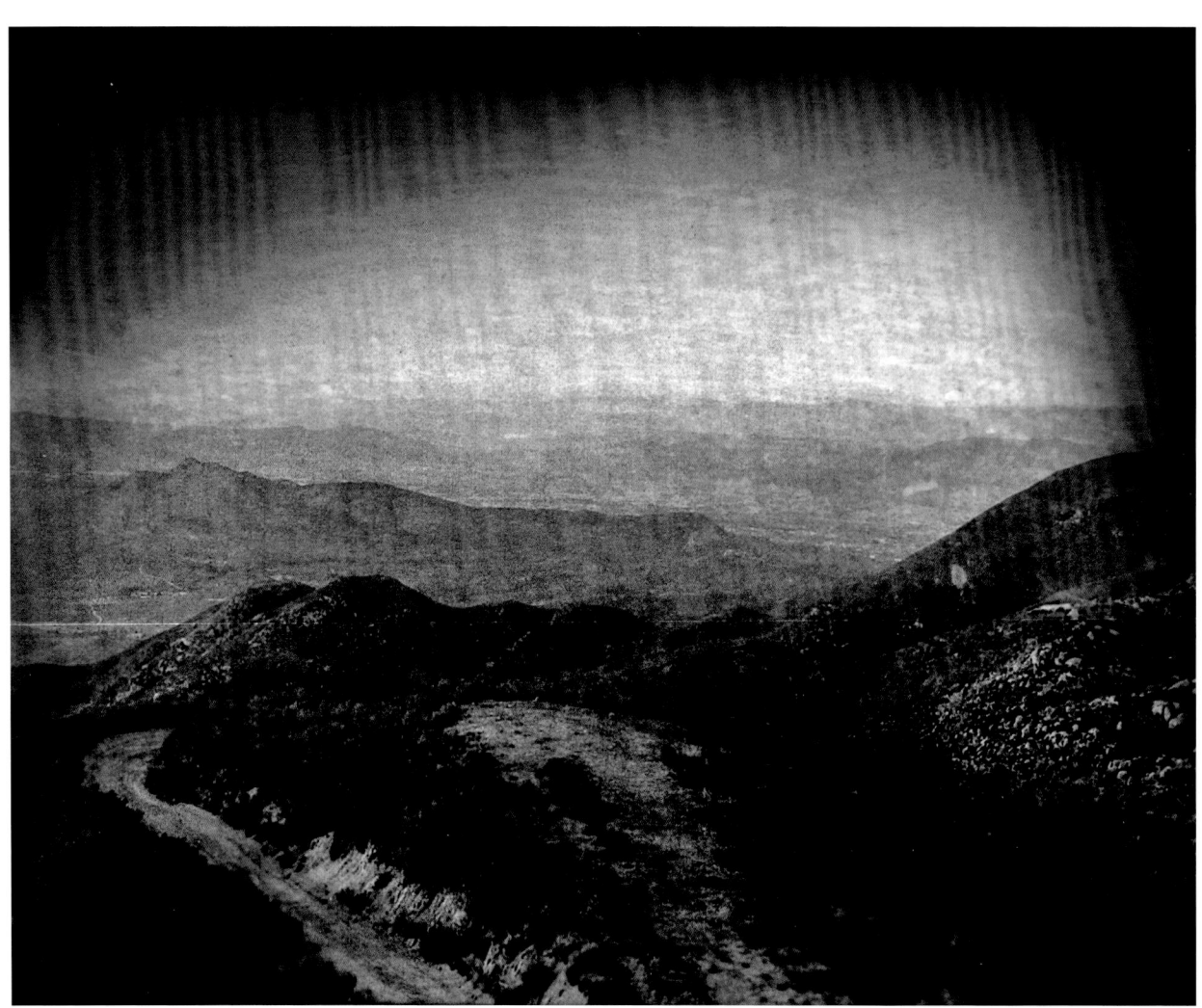

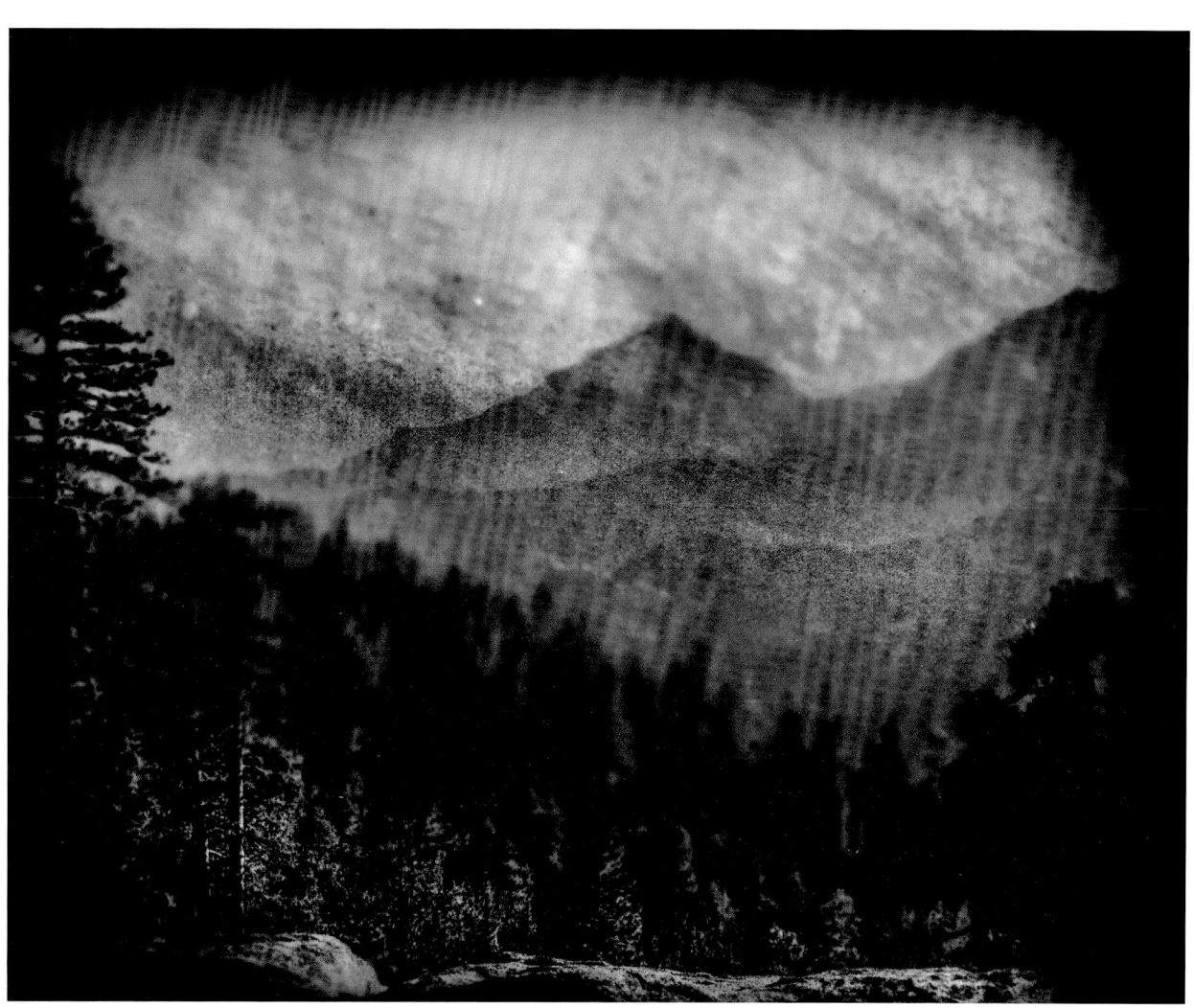

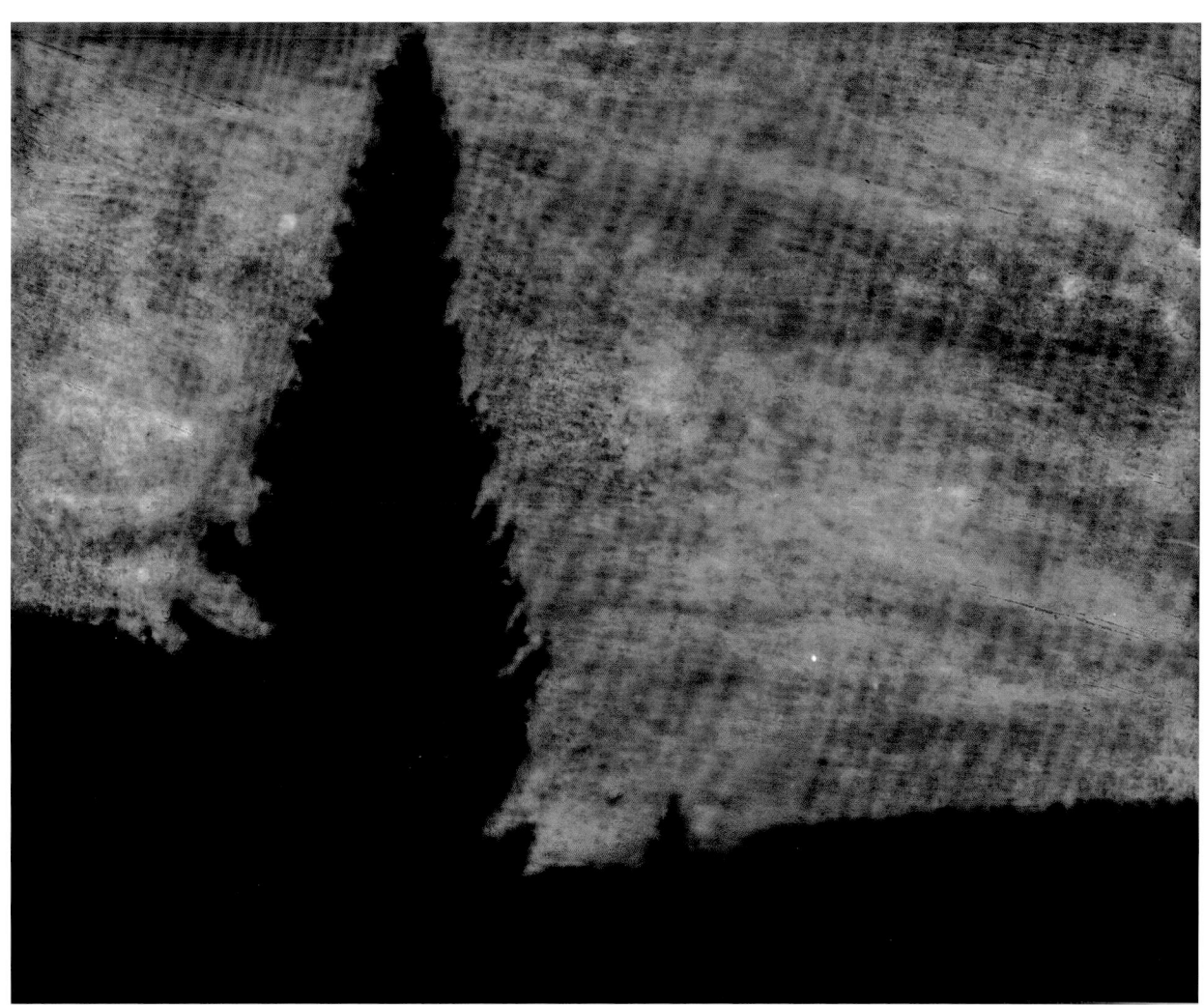

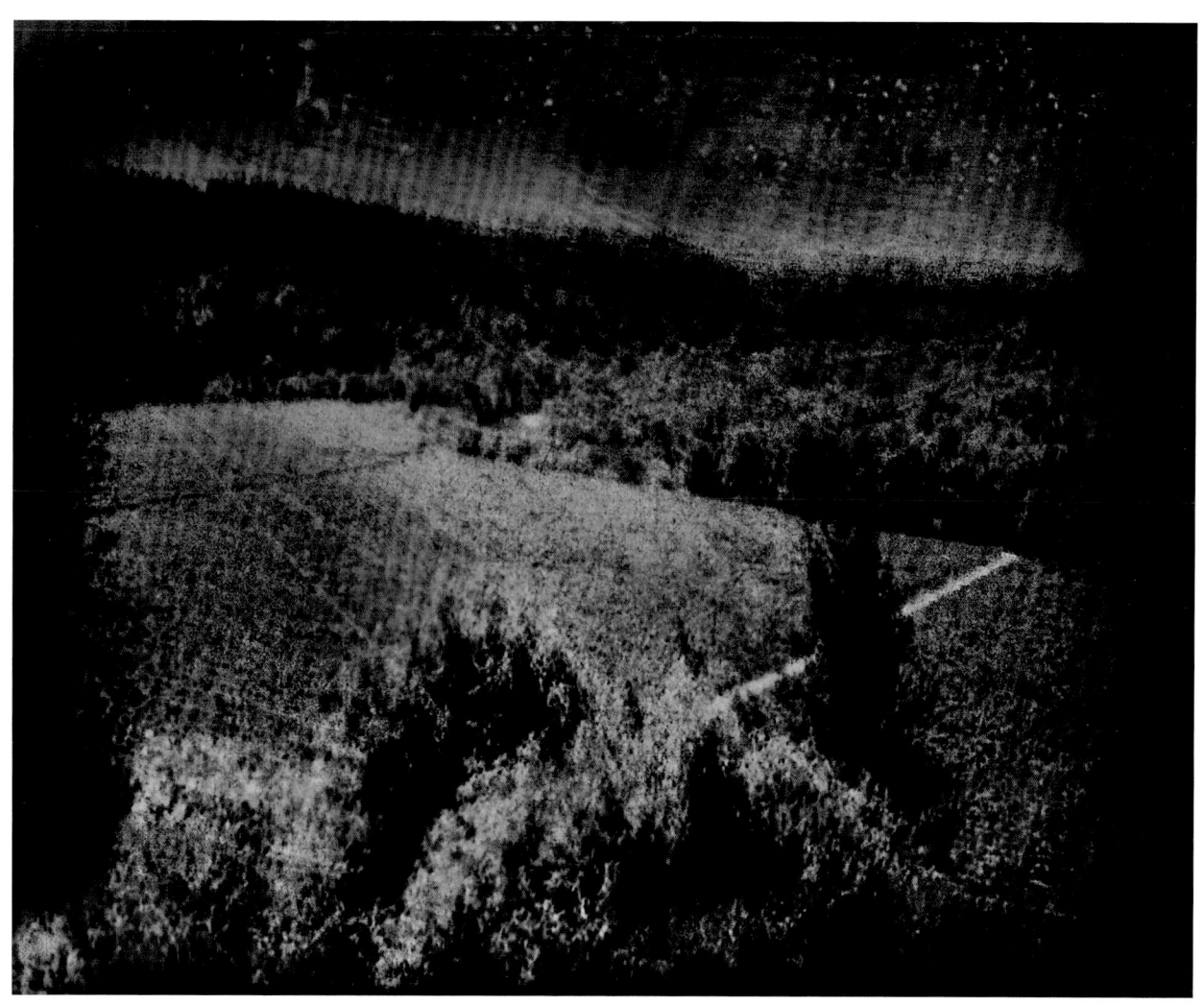

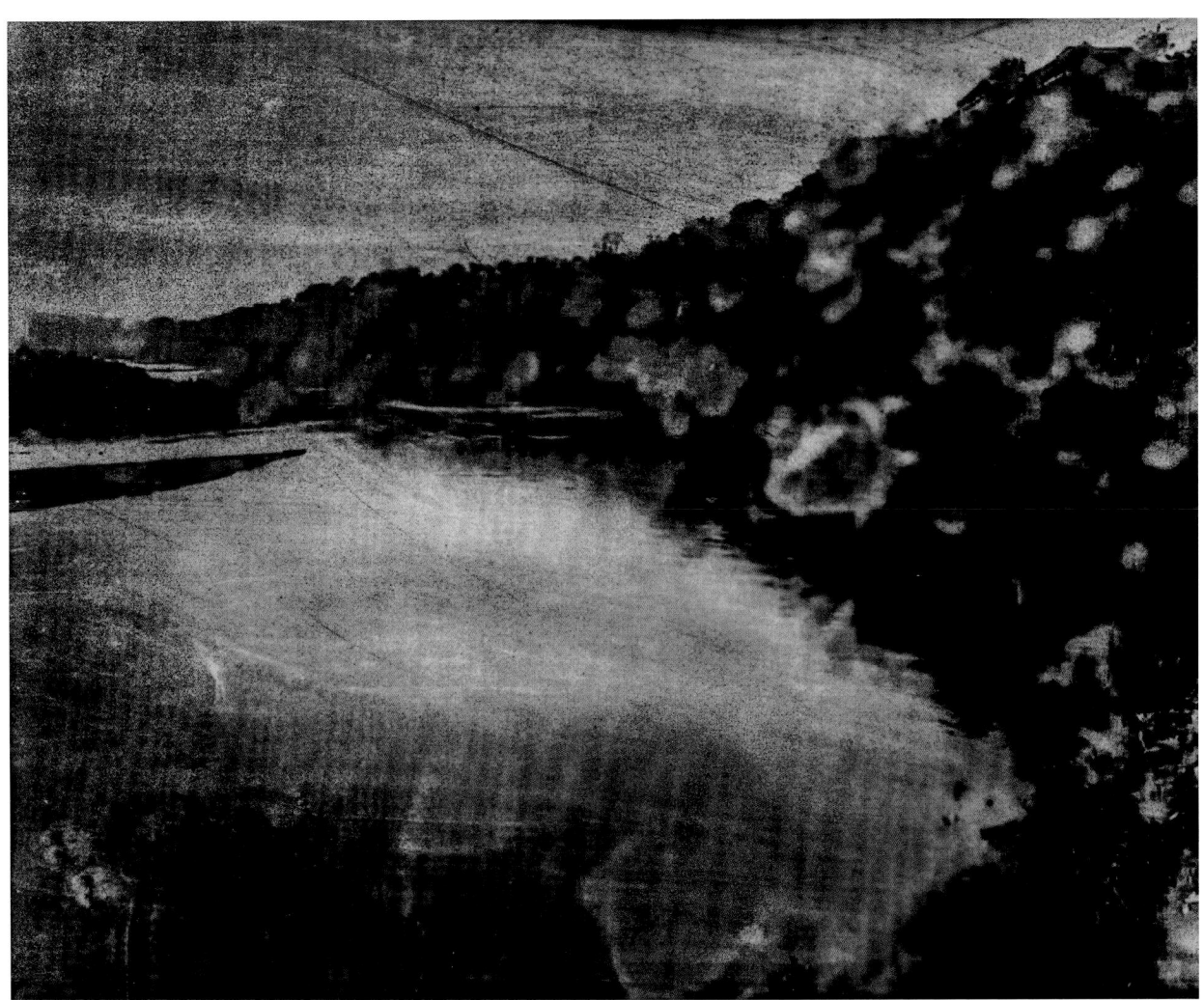

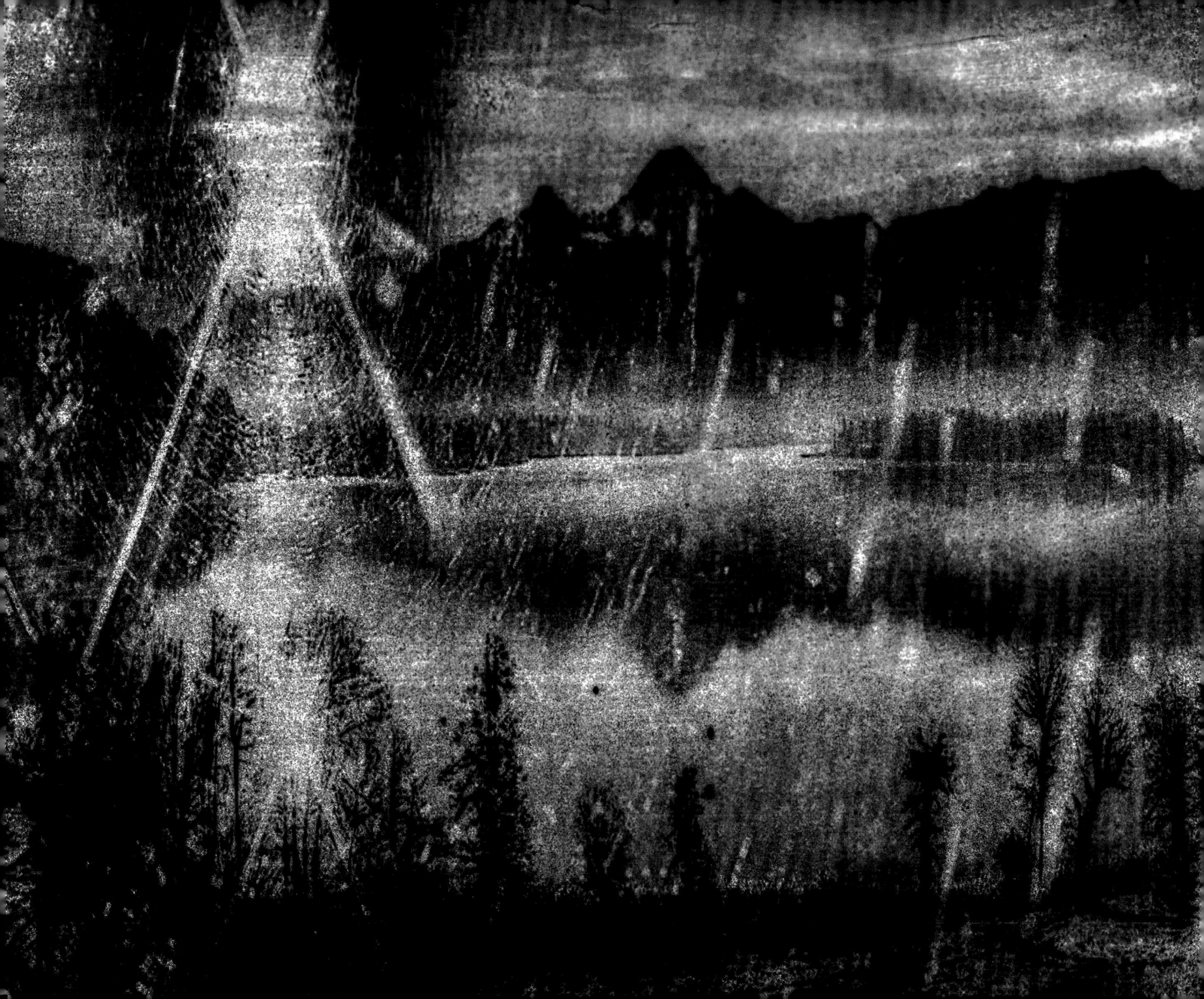

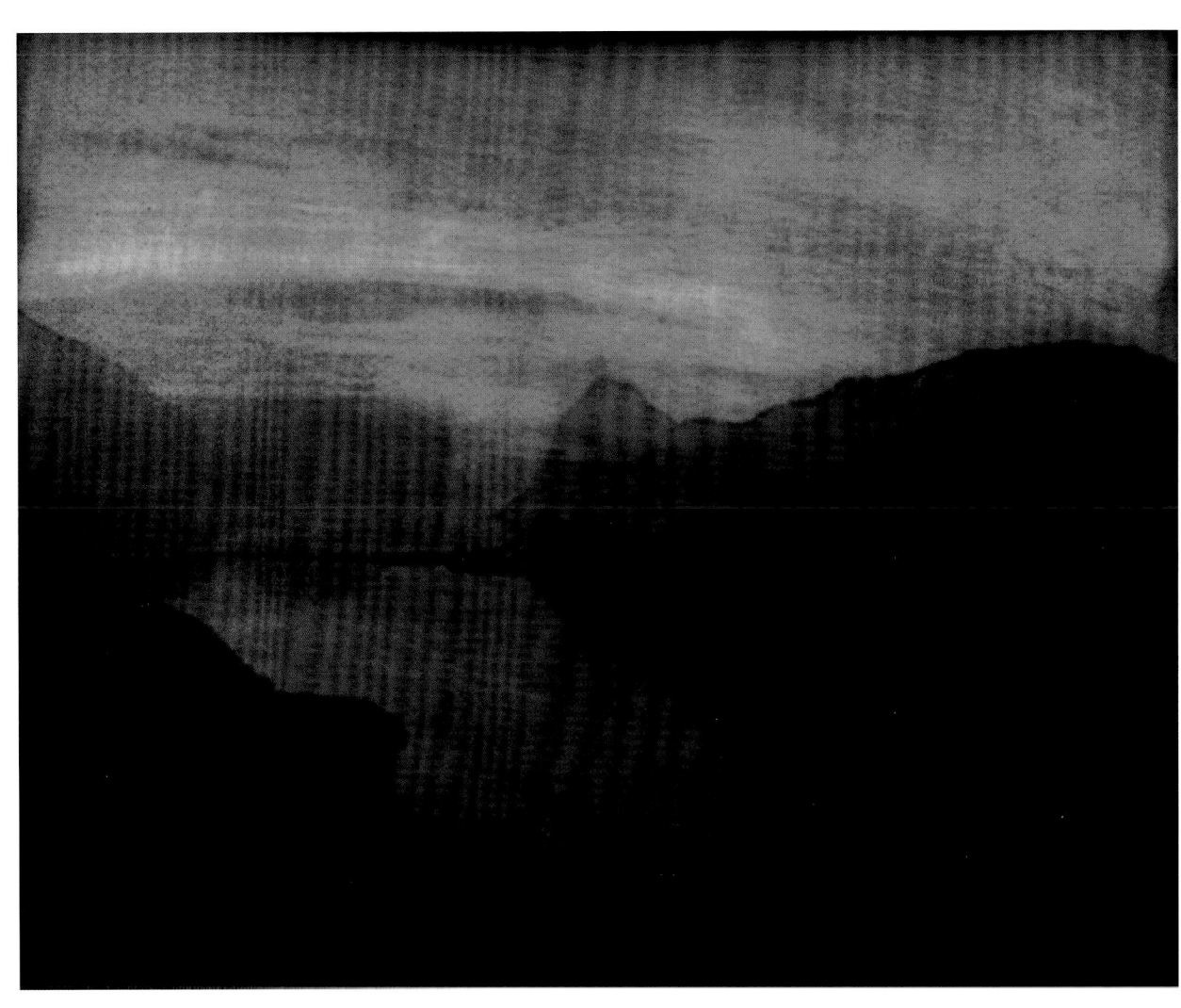

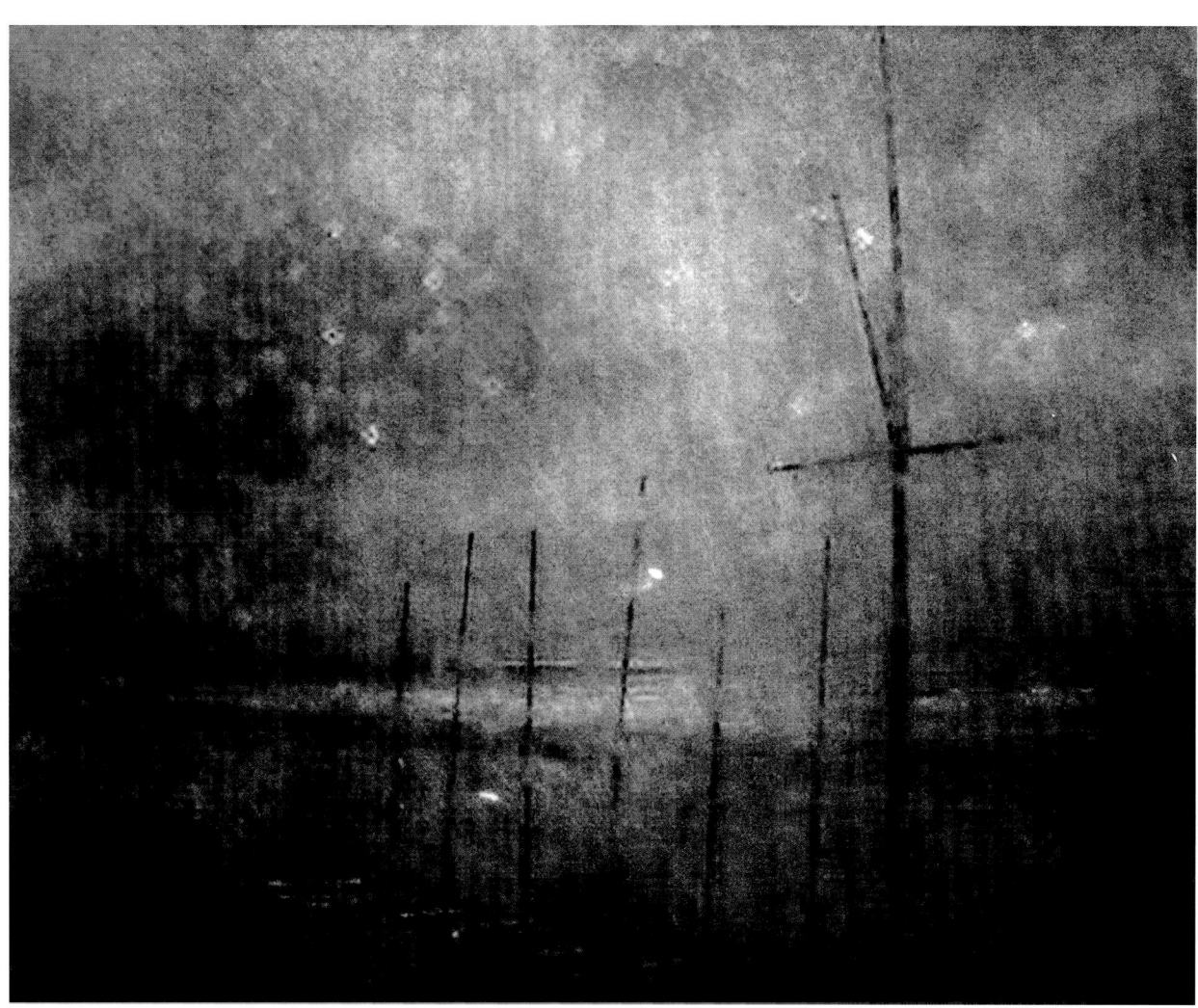

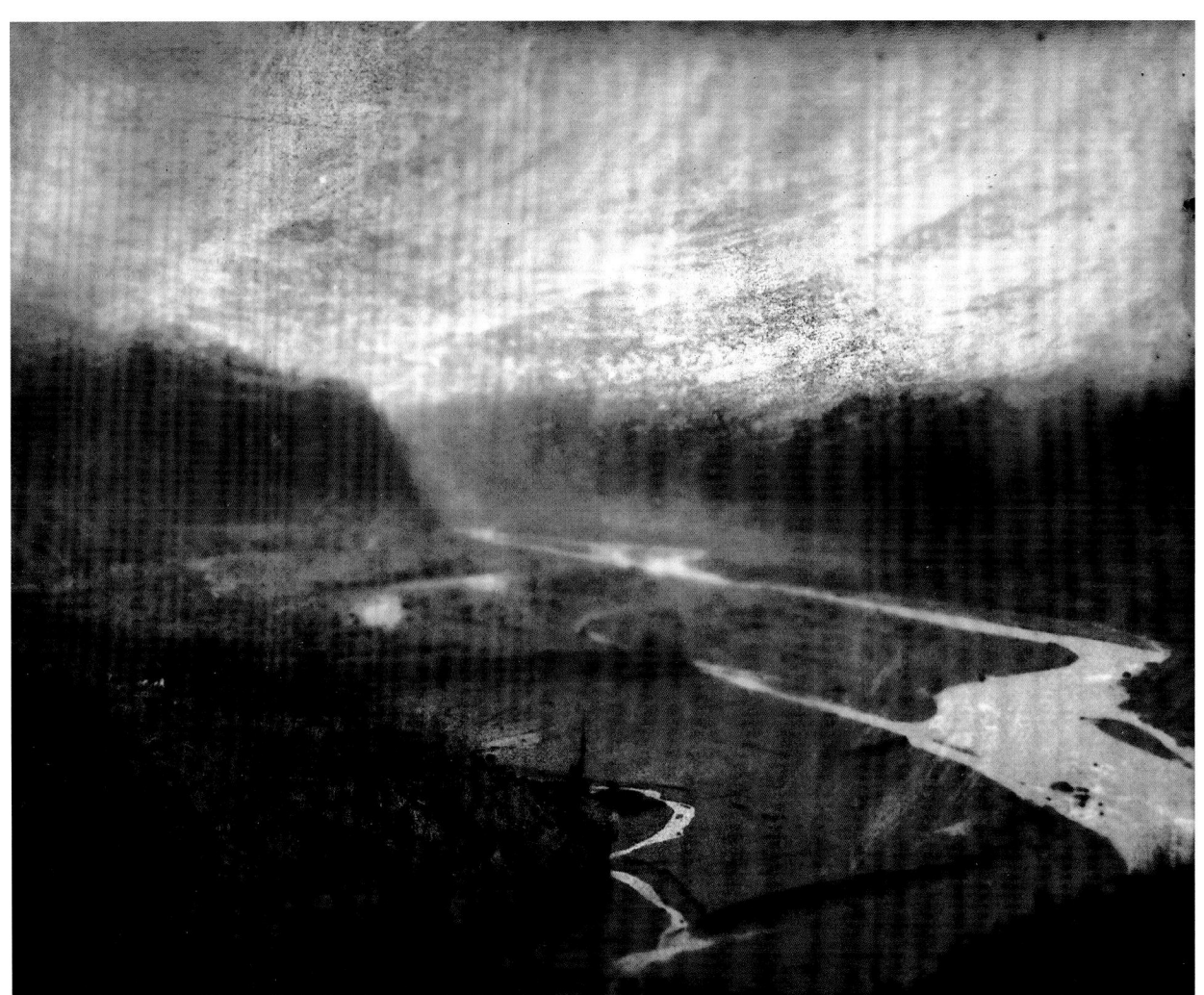

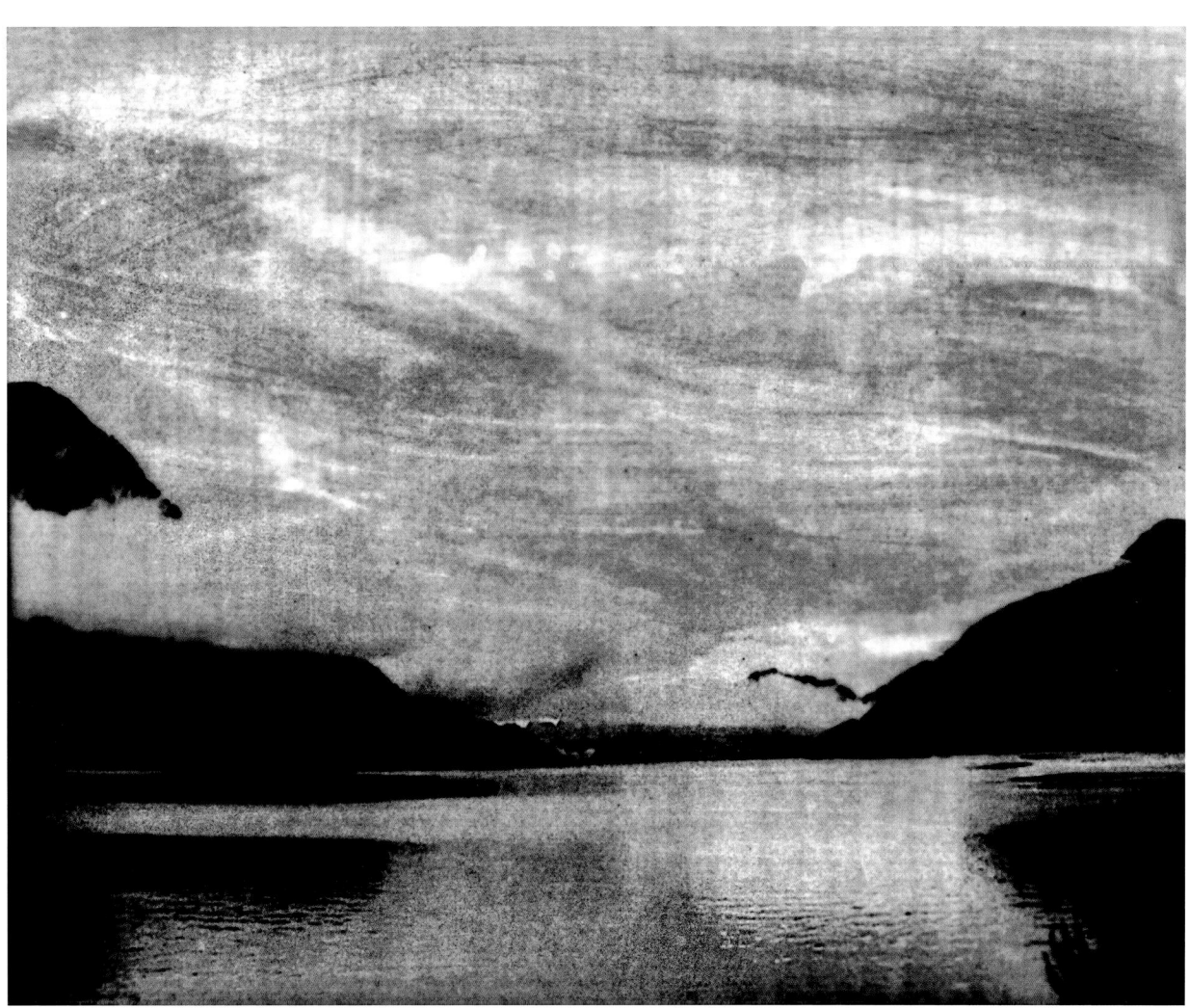

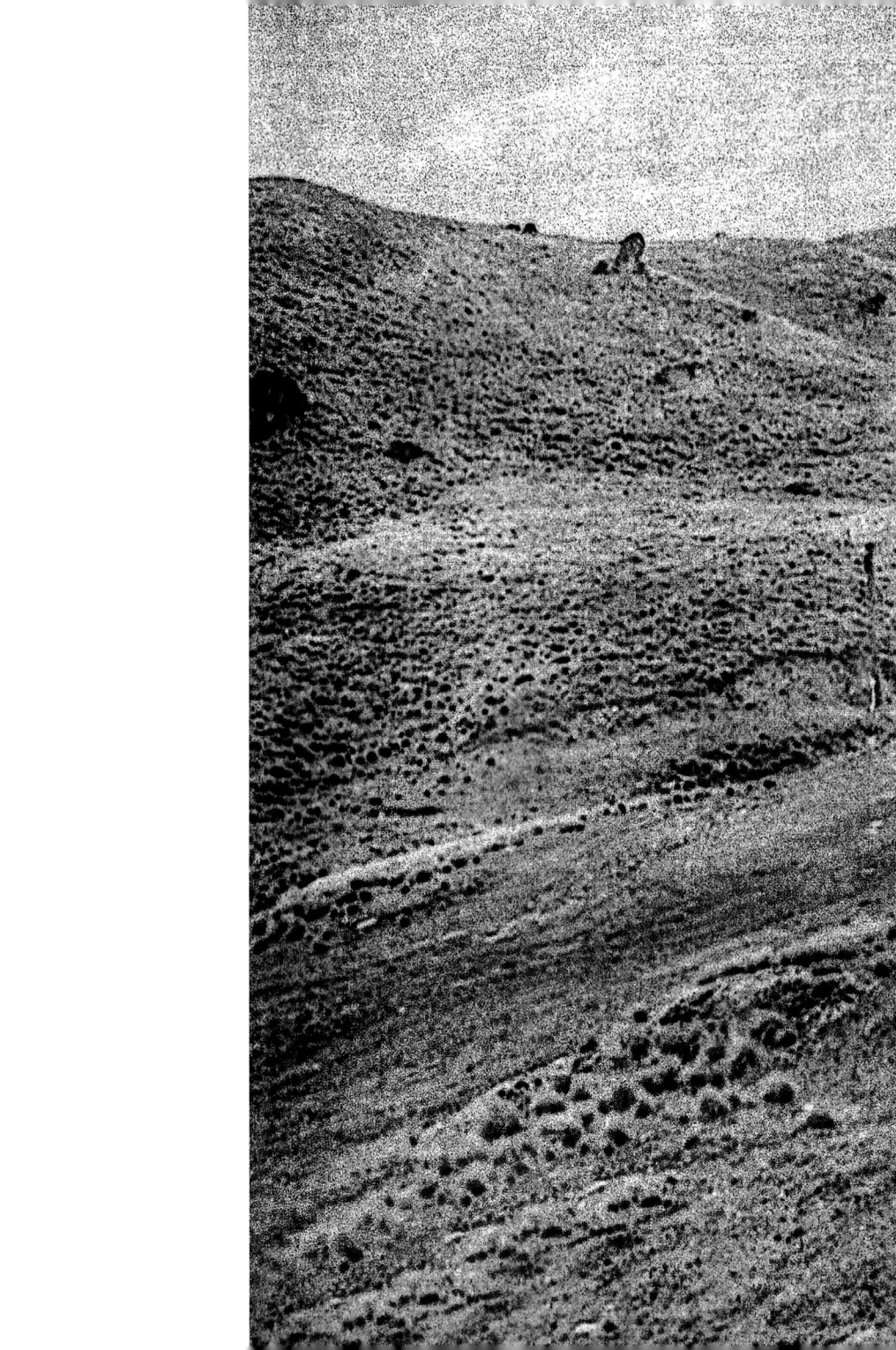

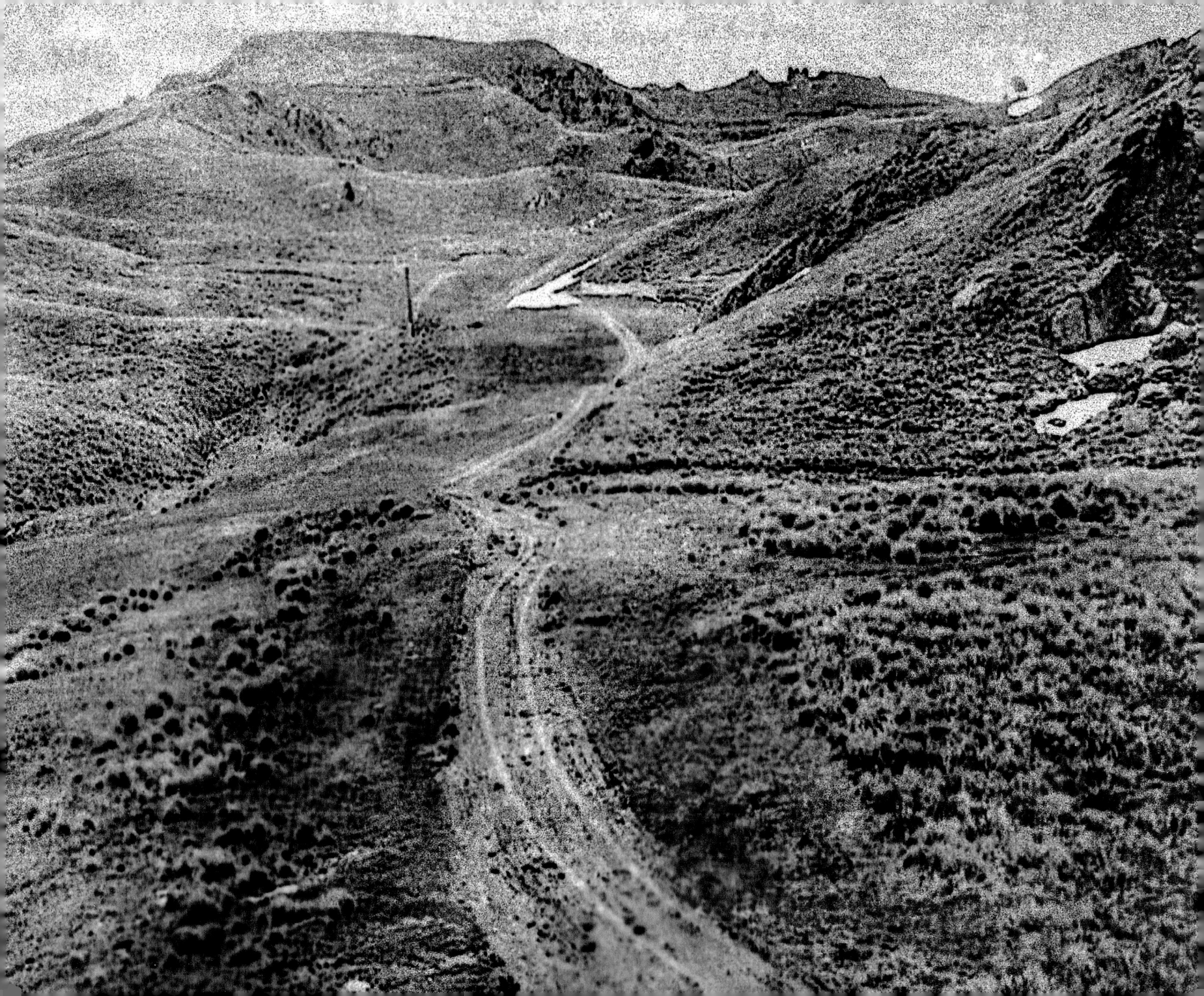

List of Plates: Coordinates

Titles for images (in order of appearance)

62.009730, -6.771640	47.710900, -124.415400	31.056899, -81.436700
48.294685, -113.241478	35.181456, 136.906386	34.161397, -117.637554
26.142350, -81.693869	39.234400, -106.817500	36.887900, -118.555100
36.112764, -113.996069	48.122900, 14.872060	47.369100, 8.001670
-43.464500, 170.017600	44.582440, 7.969640	38.610470, -122.869160
35.996611, -78.899080	44.582440, 7.969640	52.374030, 4.889690
46.979000, -103.538700	48.310900, 14.324000	0.083333 36.666664
-25.343800, 131.034700	47.799410, 13.043990	59.332580, 18.064900
40.659307, -111.920964	48.795969, -120.670387	47.183820, 7.373710
30.003540, -91.818730	18.341900, -64.930700	52.143200, -4.394850
43.094110, -73.797600	33.509720, 126.521940	48.001990, -123.600000
41.997000, -73.997400	44.797715, -110.434367	46.977860, 8.053260
-43.754000, 171.163700	47.307629, -120.082837	-44.527600, 169.126300
34.233000, 135.167000	40.681100, -111.791330	
37.874720, 127.734170	39.289801, -76.613188	

Reclaimed Landscapes:
Scenes from *No Man's Land*

By Martha A. Sandweiss

These images are not what they seem.

Look first. Well-worn trails undulate over arid rolling terrain. Boulders rise from mirror-still water; tree branches dance against featureless skies. Wind-eroded canyonlands fade into smudged horizons. Only a lonely cross, some widely spaced electrical poles, the careful banking of a road suggest people have been here before in these dark and moody landscapes.

What are we looking at exactly? Recent scenes? Something from long ago? These photographs refuse to orient us in time. Some could have been made at the dawn of the photographic age. The black-and-white tonalities, mottled skies, and out-of-focus forms all evoke the earliest landscapes from the 1840s and '50s, when photographers struggled to sensitize their daguerreian plates and glass-plate negatives in difficult out-of-doors conditions. Others remind us that the images could have been made only after construction crews arrived to carve the roads and string the electrical wires. That narrows things down only a bit. The photographs could have been made yesterday or 150 years ago.

These untitled images refuse to orient us in space, as well. At first glance, they feel familiar, evoking the landscapes made by pioneer photographers like Timothy H. O'Sullivan, Carleton Watkins, or William Henry Jackson, who hauled their heavy wet-plate cameras across the West in the years following the Civil War. In the employ of government survey teams, they sought to show Americans what the West looked like and how they might find their way through it, to rich mineral deposits, fertile farm land, or the nascent cities of the West Coast. They looked for ways to catalog the region's natural resources. With intelligence and pictorial skill, they made sense of a little-understood place and claimed it as quintessentially American.

Although their expedition leaders often dictated what they should photograph, these photographers also exercised free will. They placed their cameras just so, waited for the right light, excluded one bit of visual information in order to capture another. In their photographs, national political agendas and aesthetic sensibilities merge to convey an ordered sense of nationalistic pride. Even the emptiness of the landscapes serves a purpose at once artistic and strategic. By excluding the West's native peoples, the pictures underscore the inevitability of westward expansion and the moral righteousness of Manifest Destiny. With a visual vocabulary of studied stillness, they denote power and control. They offer proof of how the very act of photographing can confer meaning upon a place.

But my initial reading of these photographs takes me down the wrong path. I *imagine* myself in the American West here. I think I see the arid canyonlands, the dry hills of the Great Basin, the coastal boulders along the Pacific shore. I feel like I recognize that panoramic view, that landscape shot from a high reference point that proclaims the photographer (and his nation) master of all he surveys. But I'm not in the West here. At least not all of the time. It's my own preconceived ideas about landscapes that take me to that place, and slot these images into a personal archive of familiar visual referents. We *see* based on what we already *know.* When I learn that Marcus DeSieno made all of these extraordinary photographs over the past few years, without ever leaving his studio, I have to go back and look again. Knowledge changes how I see. I've been asking all the wrong questions.

DeSieno makes these pictures by hacking into surveillance cameras, closed-circuit television feeds, and the vast network of open-source web camera feeds on the Internet. Easy work, he says. From the comfort of home, he roams the globe, voraciously accessing camera feeds from city councils, tourist bureaus, government agencies, and sources I'm reluctant to ask about. He has now visited more than 15,000 camera feeds. In our global surveillance state, all of us are among the watched—just look around you at the cameras mounted on stop signs, in stores, in museums, in airports. But DeSieno has become a watcher.

His interests undermine the true purpose of the cameras he hacks. He cares nothing about the people whose behavior is ostensibly being surveilled, not the speeders, the vandals, the shoplifters, or the trespassers. He's not interested in singular moments of human drama, but rather in the vacant and empty landscapes captured more inadvertently by surveillance cameras, as they whir away waiting for something to happen.

We might ask whether landscape is even the proper word to characterize the raw image captured on a battery-operated digital camera mounted in a remote spot that operates without human intervention. The very concept of landscape implies human *perception*, what a particular person might see from a specific point of view, how they might make sense of that scene based on their knowledge, experience, and cultural values. So perhaps what the mechanically operated cameras capture cannot be termed landscapes. But the digital images become landscapes when DeSieno singles them out and looks at them anew from a quirky perspective of his own.

On his computer-aided raids of far-distant cameras, DeSieno looks for images that connote alienation, isolation, emptiness, and melancholy. He's attracted to soft-focus views, to landscapes blurred by raindrops or grimy camera lenses. He's like a picker strolling through a flea market grabbing up everything with resale potential. When he spots an online image he likes, he captures it with a computer screenshot. Eventually, he will transform these images and make them his own. But because he begins with pictures from unmanned cameras, his work implicitly challenges the idea of the photographer as a genius or master, thoughtfully capturing the world with deliberate artistic intent. Surveillance cameras captured these images incidentally, as part of a project to find something else. The images are like the wrong creatures caught up in a fishing net; the dolphin accidentally trapped in an overzealous search for tuna.

The genius here lies not in taking the photograph in the first place, but in spotting it after it has already been made, selecting it from among hundreds of thousands of other surveillance images generated in precisely the same way. Although he starts as a picker, DeSieno eventually becomes more like a curator or archivist, sifting through thousands of screenshots, searching for images that best suit his needs. He may not be taking the photographs, but he is thinking like a photographer when he makes his visual selections based on the aesthetic composition of the image, how the images will work together, and what raises interesting questions about the very meaning of landscape photography.

So he starts with a digital image and captures it by digital means. And then, determined to conceal the pixilation of the image, he turns to antique photographic processes, collapsing the whole history of photographic technology in on itself.

DeSieno uses a beautiful old wooden camera, with brass fittings, black bellows, and a plate holder large enough for a 4 x 5-inch negative. He uses a waxed paper negative process, not unlike that employed by Henry Fox Talbot, the British photographer credited with inventing the photographic negative. He brushes the light-sensitive silver emulsion onto the paper in a darkroom, adds melted wax to make the paper more translucent, and sometimes brushes on additional wax at the end. The texture of the paper fibers—so dissimilar from the smooth surface one would find on a glass or acetate negative—results in a soft image that obscures the pixelated origins of the digital original. The brushstrokes left behind by the added wax enhance the effect of a handworked image, leaving painterly streaks across the skies and blurring the outlines of the natural forms.

He sets his camera up in front of his computer screen. Old technology faces the new. A single exposure can take up to several hours to make in the darkened room.

DeSieno's laboriously made negatives can be printed only through a contact printing method, each 4 x 5 negative producing a 4 x 5 positive print. To make the exhibition-sized prints of the images in this book, he must pivot again, from a nineteenth-century process back to a modern one, scanning his positive prints into his computer and digitally printing 16 x 20– and 32 x 40–inch prints to mount on the wall. He is not just a wizard of photographic printmaking, but a time-traveling scavenger, borrowing technologies from this century or that, and modifying them to suit his needs. His prints effectively destroy the associations we have between a particular technology, a particular chronological moment, and the content of an image. That makes them unsettling.

They're similarly unsettling because for all their modernity and reliance on computer technologies, these photographs have the feel of images from the late nineteenth and early twentieth centuries, and not just because they mimic some of the technical imperfections of the earliest landscape photographs. DeSieno is a scavenger of aesthetic styles, as well as technologies. He pays homage to the Tonalist painters who used monochromatic palettes to create moody landscapes filled with shadow and abstractly rendered forms. He echoes the work of the photographic Pictorialists, who used soft-focus exposures and manipulated their negatives to assert the importance and power of the artist over the mechanical power of the camera. He borrows from the pictorial strategies of Japanese woodblock printmakers who used flat massed forms and a compressed depth of field as essential components of their landscape images. For all of these earlier artists, landscapes functioned as mirrors to the human soul. They conveyed emotion, feeling, and desire; they made outwardly visible the invisible stirrings of the spirit.

But what lurks in the soul of a surveillance camera?

Despite their homage to older pictorial styles and reliance on antique technologies, these photographs raise profound questions about our contemporary age of totalizing surveillance. The surveillance of people raises legal and moral questions about privacy, policing, the power of the state. But how do we even frame the issues that arise from surveillance-camera images of unpeopled natural spaces? Can a natural landscape have any kind of right to privacy? There's scant evidence for thinking that way in an American context. But in 2014, New Zealand passed a law declaring that the former Te Urewera National Park, a site sacred to the Maori people, would henceforth be a legal entity with "all the rights, powers, duties, and liabilities of a legal person." In 2017, the Maori won another victory when New Zealand granted the same rights to the Whanganui River, which the Maori regard as an ancestor. If we've grown used to a global world in which your human rights depend upon your citizenship, we now need to contemplate a world in which some landscapes have rights and others do not, depending on the political regimes that lay claim to them.

It's impossible to reverse engineer these landscape photographs, and figure out with any certainty just what an untended camera was doing there anyway. We can guess. It's there to prevent vandalism, catch speeders, spot trespassers. We can't know for sure. So we have to focus on the larger issues, and think about landscapes writ large, as opposed to focusing on the issues posed by any particular spot. The situation presents an odd inverse of the old adage: If a tree falls in the forest and there's no one around to hear it, does it make a sound? Here the cameras make digital image after digital image no one sees. Then DeSieno comes along and recovers them. It's a bit like racing backward in time, faster than the speed of sound, to hear the crashing tree.

In this era of the Anthropocene, when we embrace the idea that the natural world has been shaped and profoundly altered by human contact, surveillance cameras seem but one more way of shaping the natural landscape. Simply by being there, they impose a meaning. Their presence marks a space as controlled, watched, and patrolled, and defines it as a site where things might happen. A surveillance camera cannot instill fear in a place, as it can in a person. But if it cannot change how a nonsentient natural space feels, it can change how we feel about it. The presence of the camera suggests a place is vulnerable to human abuse (hence cameras protecting rock art), or conversely so powerful it can inflict danger on others (think of the cameras that monitor cliffside walks, or watch for speeders on desert highways).

For the observer, the surveillance camera invents hierarchies of value and meaning. It proclaims that what is important in any given slice of the natural world is not the unseen biological or geological processes that shape and reshape the place, but the hard-to-fathom agenda of whomever placed the all-seeing camera. It implies that what is most important will be visible. But not all important things are. Think about the many markers of climate change. By effectively rescuing the unvalued landscapes caught up in the digital surveillance of humans acting badly, DeSieno asks us to think about what these places are without us. An almost impossible task, because the surveillance cameras that provide the sources for his images are already there.

In the end, despite all the troubling issues raised here about the privatization of property and the omnipresence of the surveillance state, these pictures are also satisfyingly subversive and gloriously redemptive. DeSieno transforms images made without aesthetic intent into carefully handworked landscapes that reflect his own sensibilities. He makes the impersonal personal. And yet, although it seems paradoxical, he simultaneously makes the private public. He casts scenes not meant for wide distribution into the public sphere. In the end, it's his view of the world that will prevail. Long after the digital footage captured by the surveillance cameras is discarded or erased, DeSieno's smart and deeply moving photographs will remain.

Biographies

Ariel Shanberg is a curator and writer. From 2003 to 2015 he was the executive director at the Center for Photography at Woodstock (CPW), which, under his leadership, received numerous accolades including the 2009 Spotlight Award from the Lucie Foundation for significantly altering the landscape of photography. In addition to curating dozens of group and solo exhibitions at CPW, Ariel has organized exhibitions at The Light Factory, the Philadelphia Photo Arts Center, the Islip Art Museum, the Dorsky Museum, and the Houston Center for Photography.

His writing on the works of various artists, including Lucas Foglia, Hillerbrand+Magsamen, Jon Horvath, Jeffrey Milstein, Rachel Papo, among others, has appeared in such publications as *Aspect: The Chronicle of New Media Art*, *Contact Sheet*, *European Photography*, *Exposure*, *Nueva Luz: Photographic Journal*, and *Photograph*. Shanberg is a current member of the board of directors for the Society for Photographic Education and the advisory board of the Center for Photography at Woodstock.

Martha A. Sandweiss is a historian of the United States, with particular interests in the history of the American West, visual culture, and public history. She received her Ph.D. in History from Yale University and began her career as a photography curator at the Amon Carter Museum in Fort Worth, Texas. She later taught American Studies and History at Amherst College for twenty years before joining the Princeton University faculty in 2009.

Sandweiss is the author or editor of numerous books on American history and photography. Her publications include *Passing Strange: A Gilded Age Tale of Love and Deception Across the Color Line* (2009), a finalist for the Los Angeles Times Book Prize in History and the National Book Critics Circle Award in Biography, and *Print the Legend: Photography and the American West* (2002), winner of the Organization of American Historians' Ray Allen Billington Award for the best book in American frontier history and the William P. Clements Award. Her other works include *Laura Gilpin: An Enduring Grace* (1986), winner of the George Wittenborn Award for outstanding art book, and the coedited volume *The Oxford*

History of the American West (1994), winner of the Western Heritage Award and the Caughey Western History Prize for outstanding book on the history of the American West.

At Princeton, Sandweiss teaches courses on the history of the American West and on narrative writing, and currently heads the Princeton and Slavery Project. She serves as faculty adviser to graduate student groups working in the fields of public history and Native American studies. The recipient of grants from the National Endowment for the Humanities, the American Council of Learned Societies, and the Rockefeller Foundation, she consults widely on matters related to history education and the use of visual images for historical research and writing.

Marcus DeSieno is a lens-based artist who is interested in how the advancement of photographic technology has changed our relationship to the natural world. DeSieno often combines antiquated and obsolescent photographic processes with contemporary imaging technologies in his work to engage in a critical dialogue on the evolution of the photographic medium in relation to seeing. He received his MFA in Studio Art from the University of South Florida and is currently the Assistant Professor of Photography at Central Washington University in Ellensburg, Washington. DeSieno also serves on the board of directors for the In-Sight Photography Project, a nonprofit organization dedicated to empowering youth to communicate their unique personal visions through photography, guided by respect for individuals, communities, and cultures.

DeSieno's work has been exhibited nationally and internationally at the Aperture Foundation, Center for Fine Art Photography, Candela Gallery, the Fort Wayne Museum of Art, Rayko Photo Center, Center for Photography at Woodstock, and various other galleries and museums. His work has also been featured in a variety of publications including *The Boston Globe*, *Feature Shoot*, *GUP Magazine*, *Hyperallergic*, *Huffington Post*, *National Geographic's Proof*, *PDN*, *Slate*, *Smithsonian Magazine*, and *Wired*. DeSieno was selected for Photolucida's Critical Mass Top 50 and as an Emerging Talent by LensCulture in 2016.

Acknowledgments

This book would not be possible without the support, friendship, and assistance of many. I feel honored to have had so much help and to know I'm not alone.

First and foremost, I'd like to thank three mentors that have guided me along the way. Thank you Wendy Babcox, Noelle Mason, and John Willis. I wouldn't be an artist if it weren't for the three of you. Your friendship and direction have helped me become the person I am and I look to you still for wisdom. Having you in my life is a privilege.

I have been fortunate to have a great deal of wonderful teachers who have helped hone my craft, especially Neil Bender, John Byrd, Adam Ekberg, Gregory Green, Jason Lazarus, Allison Moore, Cathy Osman, Kate Philbrick, Anat Pollack, Tim Segar, and Wally Wilson.

To my friends who have been a rock for me in tough times and have helped me immeasurably in the creation of this work, through late night beers, heated discussion in the studio, and adventures of all sorts, I couldn't have done this without you. Thank you Will Douglas, Natalie Ivis, Mercedes Lake, Jon Notwick, and Nick Rouke.

To my friends across the country, your support means everything to me. Thank you Douglas Adams, Hilary Baker, Michael Bauman, Katina and Gary Bitsicas, Guy Cain, James Cartwright, Jeremy Chandler, Shawn Cheatham, Marielle Clark, Christine Comple, Justin Cooper, Rob Dallas, Mary Anne Escobar, Joshua Farr, Taylor Finke, Becky Flanders, Angela Franks Wells, Garth Goldwater, Jennifer Greenwell, John Hargraves, Sarah Horowitz, Sarah Howard, Samantha Johnston, Jon Jones, Eric Joyce, Daniel Kariko, Adam Keller, Bahareh Khoshooee, Katie Kohnfelder, Christos Kompogiorgas, Christopher Kwiat, Forrest Macdonald, Robyn Manning, Roberto Marquez, Rania Matar, Adam Mathieu, Deb Meadows, Nick Meyer, Ariella Miller, Michael Mirer, Greer Muldowney, Dianna Noyes, Kym O'Donnell, Thomas O'Neill, Alice Packard, Samantha Pavlic, Tristan Pease, Toni Pepe Dan, Eric Pickersgill, Scott Pierce, Taylor Pilote, Pearse Pinch, Alan Phan, Beth Plakidas, Libbi Ponce, Amanda Jeanelle Poss, Camilo Ramirez, Hillary Reed, Mary K. Reilly, Jim Reiman, Shane

Rocheleau, Selina Roman, Kristen Roles, Jack Rossiter-Munley, Sean Ryan, Jay Seawell, Gregg Schlanger, Curt Steckel, Ryan Stratton, Zach Stephens, Gordon Stettinius, Alison Terndrup, Dan Van Wormer, Joshua White, and Janett Zizumbo.

Thank you to my family, Mom, Dad, Ken, Steve, Max, Alicia, and Gabby, for your unconditional love. I know I can always count on you.

To my students I've taught over the years—thank you for the constant inspiration. Teaching is the most emotionally rewarding endeavor I've ever taken on in my life and I am glad to have shared my time with all of you.

My thanks to Marlboro College and Central Washington University for their financial support.

Thank you to Michael Itkoff, Taj Forer, Ursula Damm, and Daylight Books for your vision in making this book a reality. I am beyond grateful to Martha Sandweiss and Ariel Shanberg for their phenomenal essays.

Lastly, this book is dedicated to two beautiful souls that are no longer with us, Jaro Studencki and Lucy DeLaurentis. My closest friends, both continue to inspire me and keep me moving forward. Their memories endure through the actions of others and their impact is everlasting.